Powell & Moya

Twentieth Century Architects

Powell & Moya

Twentieth Century Architects

Kenneth Powell

THE
TWENTIETH
CENTURY
SOCIETY

ENGLISH HERITAGE

RIBA **Publishing**

© Kenneth Powell, 2009
Published by RIBA Publishing, 15 Bonhill Street, London EC2P 2EA

ISBN 978 1 85946 303 1

Stock Code 67452

British Library Cataloguing in Publications Data
A catalogue record for this book is available from the British Library

Publisher: Steven Cross
Commissioning Editor: Lucy Harbor
Project Editor: Susan George
Editor: Ian McDonald
Designed & typeset by Carnegie Book Production
Printed and bound by The Charlesworth Group, Wakefield

RIBA Publishing is part of RIBA Enterprises Ltd.
www.ribaenterprises.com

Front cover photo: The Skylon on its riverside site
Back cover photo: Philip Powell and Hidalgo Moya
Frontispiece photo: St John's College, Cambridge

Foreword

Powell and Moya burst onto the post-war British architectural scene with two spectacular competition wins: one for the Churchill Gardens housing estate on the River Thames at Pimlico (1946), and the other for the Skylon at the Festival of Britain on London's South Bank (1950). Philip Powell and Hidalgo 'Jacko' Moya were only in their late twenties, barely out of the AA school of architecture, yet both projects have stood the test of time like few others. The Pimlico housing estate, which has always been prized by Westminster Council, has proved to be highly popular, and there are continuous calls to rebuild the Skylon – 'London's lost icon'.

By the time I joined their practice in 1973, they were already established as being among the great and the good, with designs for colleges in Oxford and Cambridge and some of the best hospitals in the country under their belt. The practice went on to win the Queen's Royal Gold Medal in 1974 and Philip Powell was knighted, made a Companion of Honour of the Order of Merit and became a stalwart of both the Royal Fine Art Commission and the Royal Academy.

The secret of their success was that they were extremely gifted architects and fabulous partners. They were very different characters, but totally supportive of each other. The mercurial Jacko, allegedly the son of a South American riverboat gambler and inventor (his father invented the Moya typewriter, a precursor of the IBM golf ball but with a cylinder rather than a ball), went on to become an ingenious engineer. With the Skylon he invented 'high-tech', and backed it up with the cable-suspended British pavilion at Expo 70. Yet he was also a sublime artist, had a natural 'eye' for proportion and could use stone, brick, timber and lead. He was as shy as he was talented, and wore his father's huge diamond ring with the gem facing his palm lest he be thought brash. He told me that his most important achievement in his early career was to find Philip Powell.

Philip was simply the brightest man I ever met, and one of the nicest. He was at home with mandarins from Whitehall and Oxbridge philosophers, as well as artists and architects. An English gentleman who could have passed for a scout master at a public school, his fertile, imaginative mind raced ahead of ours when we discussed the next building on the boards. His famous ten-inch roll of detail paper was quickly filled with his characteristic coloured felt-tip pen sketches exhaustively exploring the alternatives. 'Let's look at the options, regardless of merit,' he would often say with endless curiosity and energy. Sectional perspectives were his favourite and could be dashed off in minutes. He worshipped Jacko and although they worked on different projects (Philip on many more than Jacko), he would often call him in to consult. He trusted Jacko's judgement implicitly; and Jacko trusted his.

Free from whimsy or fashion, Powell & Moya's architecture is full of integrity, creativity and, in the end, has a classic beauty. Their reputation will grow with time as new generations discover their work, not least because of this long overdue book.

Jack Pringle

Acknowledgements

It was the late Philippa Powell who encouraged me to write this book and it would not have happened without her. Philippa's children, Ben and Dido, have been supportive throughout, as has Jeannie Moya, Jacko's widow.

My first acquaintance with Powell & Moya came only in 1996 when Paul Finch commissioned me to write an extended account of the practice's work for the *AJ*. Sadly, Jacko Moya had died several years before, but Philip Powell gave me an insight into its work which is fundamental to everything I have written here.

Among former partners, directors and staff members of Powell & Moya, Roger Burr, Richard Burton, Jack Pringle, Peter Skinner, Bernard Stilwell, Derek Stow and Bernard Throp have been immensely generous in providing reminiscences and reflections on the work of the firm. I owe a vast debt of gratitude to John Haworth and Jill Sheridan for making available to me the archive of material now in their possession and for providing space in their house in which to study it. The book could not have been written without their help.

Among others who have provided invaluable help are Brian Anderson (Purcell Miller Tritton), Elizabeth Boardman (Brasenose College, Oxford), Jim Cadbury-Brown, Professor Joe Mordaunt Crook, Judith Curthoys (Christ Church, Oxford), Adam Hogg, Stephen Mullin, Jan Scriven (Wolfson College, Oxford), Malcolm Underwood (St John's College, Cambridge), Dr Robin Walker (Queens' College, Cambridge) and Richard Wildman (Bedford Modern School). The idea for this book and for the series of which it forms a part came from Martin Cherry and Elain Harwood of English Heritage and Alan Powers of the Twentieth Century Society and I am grateful to them for their encouragement and advice. James Davies of English Heritage took the excellent new photographs of some of Powell & Moya's best buildings. The staff of the RIBA Library and Drawings Collection provided their usual expert service. Special thanks are due to Robert Elwall of the RIBA Library Photographic Collection.

Finally, I am grateful to Matthew Thompson of RIBA Publishing for taking up the idea of the book and to Lucy Harbor, Susan George and Anna Walters for seeing it through to publication.

Kenneth Powell, 2009

"Without the Twentieth Century Society an entire chapter of Britain's recent history was to have been lost. It was alert when others slept. It is still crucial!"

Simon Jenkins, writer, historian, journalist

Love it or hate it, the architecture of the twentieth century has shaped our world: bold, controversial, and often experimental buildings that range from the playful Deco of seaside villas to the Brutalist concrete of London's Hayward Gallery.

Arguably the most vibrant, dynamic and expressive period of architecture in history, the twentieth century generated a huge range of styles. You don't have to love them all to believe that the best of these exciting buildings deserve to be protected, just like the masterpieces of the Victorian era, many likewise once thought to be eyesores. Buildings that form the fabric of our everyday life — office blocks, schools, flats, telephone boxes, department stores — are often poorly understood.

The campaign to protect the best of architecture and design in Britain from 1914 onwards is at the heart of the Twentieth Century Society. Our staff propose buildings for listing, advise on restoration and help to find new uses for buildings threatened with demolition. Tragedies like the recent demolition of modernist house Greenside, however, show how important it is to add your voice to the campaign.

Join the Twentieth Century Society, and not only will you help to protect these modern treasures, you will also gain an unrivalled insight into the groundbreaking architecture and design that helped to shape the century.

THE
TWENTIETH
CENTURY
SOCIETY

www.c20society.org.uk

Contents

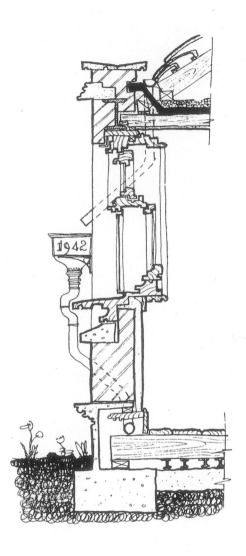

½ . FULL SIZE   12.42
                       9·45

Philip Powell's comical drawing of a drainage system featured on the programme cover for the AA's Christmas pantomime in 1942

Introduction

'They have an uncanny and seemingly uncontrived ability to sense the mood of place and time – and client,' wrote Reyner Banham of Powell and Moya in 1974.[1] The partnership had just won the Royal Gold Medal for Architecture, the first time that the prized award had gone to a practice rather than an individual. It seemed an inevitable new chapter in a success story that began when Philip Powell and Hidalgo ('Jacko') Moya, fresh out of the AA and still in their mid twenties, won the competition for Churchill Gardens in 1946. The massive housing scheme, with accommodation for 6,000 residents, took 15 years to build. In the interim, they had been responsible for the structure that, for most people, epitomised the 1951 Festival of Britain – the Skylon. They had been at the forefront of new hospital design in Britain and had built extensively in both Oxford and Cambridge, with projects that were symbols of the belated triumph of Modernism at those ancient universities. The commission to design the British Pavilion at the 1970 Osaka Expo provided more than a hint that Powell and Moya were well placed to challenge Basil Spence's role as the establishment's favoured architect (Spence died in 1976). In 1974, Powell & Moya's Museum of London was under construction and a year later the practice was commissioned to design the Queen Elizabeth II Conference Centre, close to Westminster Abbey. For nearly 30 years, the firm was in the enviable position of being able to decline jobs which it felt it could not devote sufficient time to – more than once, potential commissions were passed on to worthy young firms. Philip Powell, whose taste for public and professional service contrasted with Moya's highly private personality, was appointed to the Royal Fine Art Commission, made a Royal Academician and (in 1975) knighted. More than a decade after the demise of Powell & Moya, the practice's reputation remains strong. It is not difficult to recall the great days of the 1950s and 60s, when, it was said, there was only one sensible choice for an ambitious newly qualified British architect: to work either for the London County Council (LCC) – which then ran the largest design office in Europe – or for Powell & Moya.

Banham's 1974 *New Society* article was headed up 'Nice, modern and British!', a characterisation of Powell & Moya's work that could be seen as ambivalent. Banham's critical vision was anything but parochial. He had been the prophet of the New Brutalism, promoting the work of the Smithsons and James Stirling. By the mid seventies, his attention was turning to the work of Foster and Rogers, the new stars on the British (and soon world) scene. Was the adjective he applied to Powell & Moya – 'gentlemanly' – entirely complimentary? The practice's work was, he wrote, about 'niceties of professional gesture, rather than grand gestures' – for the latter, one

MR. J. H. MOYA (left) and Mr. Arnold Powell, winners of the Westminster City Council's housing competition.

Philip Powell (right) and Hidalgo Moya

turned to Lasdun or the Smithsons. Powell & Moya's buildings were the ones 'you didn't notice'. More recently, Alan Powers has located the firm's work as belonging to 'a middle way between the simplifications of high modernism and the reactionaries opposed to it', a tendency which had emerged in Britain during the 1930s.[2]

Powell & Moya's skill at designing for a specific context – identifying 'the character-behind-the-style of their surroundings' as Banham put it – remains the most memorable aspect of their work. In this respect, the various Oxbridge projects, most notably those at St John's in Cambridge and at Brasenose and Christ Church in Oxford, remain the most characteristic element of the practice's legacy. Yet it would be mistaken to identify Powell & Moya's work as peculiarly British (or English) and to ignore its cosmopolitan roots. Moya's free-thinking inventiveness, doubtless inherited from his Mexican-born father, was a fundamental driving force of the office. There were occasions, former practice members recall, when, frustrated by the inability of manufacturers to produce the component required for a project, Moya retired to his workshop and personally fabricated it. Powell – with cultural roots in the public schools, Oxbridge and the Church of England – had rejected the career his family favoured, travelled in Europe on the eve of the Second World War and seen the work of Corbusier and Gropius at first hand. Visiting Rotterdam soon after the end of the war, he had seen Oud's Kiefhoek, with its streets of two-storey houses, and found it 'lively, exciting, unsentimental, truly urban, neighbourly, with families near the ground and with their own gardens'.[3] The Kiefhoek embodied a vision of the modern city far removed, for example, from that seen in the LCC's highly Corbusian Roehampton Estate. Dutch Modernism undoubtedly influenced the architecture of Churchill Gardens, but it was in the later Gospel Oak housing (as Ian Nairn perceptively noted) that, in Powell's words, 'a more coherent urban pattern' emerged. Powell welcomed the fact that the houses at Gospel Oak 'bristle with life and overgrown gardens and garden sheds and washing and everyday mess'.[4]

There was something of Philip Powell's own personality in those words. For more than half a century, he and his wife Philippa lived in a large Victorian house in Kensington's Little Boltons, seeing in that time a long run-down street transformed into a billionaires' row. Their house, with its neglected garden and altered fenestration, contrasting boldly with its immaculately restored neighbours, many of them locked behind high-security gates and protected by surveillance cameras. The house had, in effect, been a multi-occupied commune for young architects before it became the Powells' family home. To the end, it remained defiantly unfashionable, with a kitchen dating back to the sixties. Behind Philip Powell's highly organised, professionally polished facade, there was a deeply artistic spirit. However, it was Powell – an outstanding, intuitive designer – who made the practice work as a business, sometimes frustrated by Moya's less punctilious approach but always certain that the latter's brilliance was fundamental to its success. Like every great architectural practice, Powell & Moya thrived on successful teamwork. The office was never large – around 50 people at most. In its early years, recruits who were used to the stiff formality of more conventional firms, in which partners were superior beings insulated behind the doors of their private offices, were amazed by its informality – jazz records on the gramophone and glasses of wine on offer at the end of the working day. A series of partners, the first of them Peter Skinner, were brought in to share in the direction of the practice. Outstanding assistants were given their head on key projects – Richard Burton, later of Ahrends Burton Koralek, for example, at Brasenose College, Oxford.

In contrast to some long-established partnerships, Powell & Moya survived the retirement of its founding principals (only to succumb to the consequences of the Private Finance Initiative). It was the collaborative nature of the practice that allowed its work to evolve and change. Although both Powell and Moya retained a firm hold on projects to the time of their retirement, they encouraged this process and the result was a dynamism that produced, for example, the outstanding hospital projects at Hastings and Maidstone.

Where once-firmly Modernist British practices such as GMW, RHWL and even YRM strayed into Postmodernism during the 1980s, Powell & Moya resisted the temptations of applied ornament and historical reference in order to produce buildings that were resolutely practical and rational. Those other practices, of course, benefited from the commercial building boom of the eighties. Powell and Moya remained reluctant to enter an arena long dominated by unashamedly commercial architects such as Fitzroy Robinson and Richard Seifert. The office slab on London Wall, part of the Museum of London project, was a building that Powell frankly disliked. His outlook, like that of so many architects of his generation, was left of centre with a passionate commitment to the public sector. Philip Powell's and Jacko Moya's retirement from practice happened at a time when Thatcherism had largely undermined the ideological – and funding – base on which much of the work of that generation depended.

Powell & Moya built few bespoke private houses; their best work embodied a strong sense of community, whether it was that of a college or a housing estate. The hospital projects for example, from Swindon through to those of the 1990s, are characterised by generous social spaces, often with a clear connection to external space. Philip Powell, reflecting on Churchill Gardens many years after its completion, felt that the development had 'too much road'. Yet it is the balance of streets and green space, a new take on the mix that underpins Georgian London, which makes the place so enjoyable and inhabitable – somewhere to live through choice, not circumstance.

Philip Powell (right) and Hidalgo Moya with a model of the British Pavilion (October 1968)

In the more than 50 years of its existence, Powell & Moya never produced a compre-hensive account of its projects and philosophy. Today, when architectural practices a few years old feel the need to commission costly monographs, that may seem surprising – but the culture of architecture has changed, and self-promotion is now the fashion. When Paul Finch, then editor of the *Architects' Journal*, asked me, back in 1996, to write a long piece on the history of Powell & Moya, I was conscious that I would be writing about a practice with a legendary reputation. However, it was also a lively and youthful practice – one could not have imagined that it would be defunct a year later. To my enormous regret, I never met Jacko Moya (who had died in 1994) – though Philip Powell's reminiscences brought him vividly to life. It was only after Philip's own death that the idea of this book emerged – encouraged by his widow, and my friend, Philippa Powell. Many people have helped in many ways in its production, and they are acknowl-edged elsewhere.

This book appears at a time when the legacy of modern architecture in Britain remains a subject of intense debate. Demolishing any building with a useful future is rarely sensible, but there is a genuine public reaction against the 'eyesores' of the recent past. However, English Heritage's listing programme for post-war buildings, and the campaigning activities of the Twentieth Century Society, have highlighted the positive qualities of the best work of the post-war era. Innovation and experiment always involve an element of danger. Some of Powell and Moya's best-known buildings – those at Brasenose College and Christ Church in Oxford and the Cripps Building at St John's, Cambridge, for instance – have been the subject of costly repair programmes, largely as a result of failed flat roofs. Today, with flat-roofing technology transformed, there is every prospect that those buildings will remain sound into the next century. Other buildings by the practice have been destroyed (the Swindon hospital and several of the private houses) or altered beyond recognition (Mayfield School) before they could be protected by listing. Nonetheless, most of Powell & Moya's buildings remain used and enjoyed – the Cripps Building now seems as much a natural part of the Cambridge scene as its medieval, Tudor, Georgian and Victorian neighbours.

British architecture is currently emerging from a period in which 'grand gestures' – or 'iconic buildings' – were back in fashion, and their appropriateness to their context was not always adequately considered. Now there is a return to the practical and the appropriate – witness, for instance, recent housing by Sergison Bates or Peter Barber. In this light, Powell & Moya's contextual Modernism acquires a new relevance. This book sets out to place the practice's work in its historical context in a period of British history extending from the end of the Second World War to the advent of New Labour. It will also hopefully interest and inspire a new generation of architects who want to build in a modern way – in tune with the city and countryside, and in the service of people. It was that vision which drove Powell & Moya's architecture: a vision still relevant today.

Notes

1   Reyner Banham, 'Nice, modern and British!', *New Society*, 18 July 1974, pp160–1.
2   Alan Powers, *Britain: Modern Architectures in History* (London, 2007), p92.
3   Philip Powell, 'Architects' approach to architecture', *RIBA Journal*, March 1966, pp120–1.
4   Ibid., p121.

CHAPTER ONE:
Churchill Gardens and After

The practice of Powell & Moya was established in 1946. On 20 May that year, Philip Powell and Hidalgo Moya, aged respectively 25 and 26 and graduates of the Architectural Association School of Architecture in London, learned that they had won an open international competition, launched in the previous year, for the design of a very large housing development for Westminster Council. The premium was £700, but far more significant was the opportunity to build a development costed at over £2 million. The 12-hectare (30-acre) site, which had been earmarked for possible redevelopment during the 1930s, was close to the Thames in Pimlico and across the river from Battersea Power Station. The streets of Victorian housing there, then regarded as anything but fashionable and punctuated by industrial and commercial premises, had been ravaged by wartime bombing. A partnership was quickly formed in order to begin phased construction of a scheme that took 15 years to build, with its 1,661 dwellings eventually housing up to 6,000 people.

The competition win was a triumph for two barely qualified young architects. 'Our first emotion was that of disbelief, later followed by surprise, joy and excitement,' Philip Powell recalled more than half a century later.[1] There had been 64 entries, assessed by Stanley Ramsey who, in partnership with S. D. Adshead from 1911, had designed the housing on the Duchy Estate in Kennington, a highly intelligent reworking of the stock-brick vernacular of Georgian London. The London boroughs had been instructed by the government to prepare plans for new housing to meet the demands of the post-war capital. (It was not until 1950 that the LCC Architect's Department began designing housing.) Churchill Gardens, as 'the Pimlico housing scheme' subsequently became known, spearheaded Westminster's efforts. The competition brief, Philip Powell recalled, was 'brilliant and concise: it encouraged adventure, as well as the more pious virtues of caution'. The Council had decided to concentrate its housing campaign on one large site rather than a number of plots scattered across its territory. The County of London Plan of 1943 suggested that development on this site, with its proximity to the river, could be dense: the maximum 200 persons per acre (equivalent to 80 persons per hectare) permitted by the Plan. This meant building high – up to the maximum nine storeys allowed in London at the time. According to Philip Powell, 'if the Council was

Opposite: The accumulator tower at Churchill Gardens, with Battersea Power Station, source of heat for the estate, in the background

Philip Powell standing on top of one of the blocks at Churchill Gardens

shocked at having been landed with two reasonably inexperienced young architects it failed to show it; it just encouraged them, argued with them and supported them, and all who worked with them over the next 15 years or so'.[2]

The two founding partners in Powell & Moya were very different characters from very different backgrounds. Arnold Joseph Philip Powell was born on 15 March 1921, at 35 Shakespeare Road, Bedford. His father, Arnold (b.1882), educated at Trinity College, Cambridge, was at the time headmaster of Bedford Modern School and was a scholarly, if slightly pedantic, figure, though not without a touch of humour. Arnold ('Archie') Powell – whose career had already included posts at Holt in Norfolk, Grantham, Sedbergh and Skipton – moved on a year later to become headmaster of Epsom College in Surrey, a minor public school, where his son became a pupil. He took holy orders, and after retirement from Epsom at the age of 57 became incumbent of the Sussex Downland parishes of Graffham and Lavington (he was known in the family as 'Hector the Rector'). He was not, it seems, particularly successful as a parish priest but was given a canonry in the cathedral city of Chichester in 1947, where he reappears in the history of Powell & Moya.

Philip Powell (knighted in 1975 and made a Companion of Honour in 1984, the first architect to receive that award) was destined, if his father had had his way, to go up to Cambridge. He had a gift for languages, and his relatively affluent background allowed him to travel in Europe as a young man. Powell had always had a huge admiration for his elder brother, Michael (b.1916), who had also qualified at the AA and who in fact joined Powell & Moya on his demob from the army late in 1946, staying until 1950. Philip Powell was quoted as saying that if his brother had been a circus clown, he would have been the same – and it was the latter's decision to become an architect that had initially led him to read up on the subject. Travelling abroad on the eve of the Second World War, the young Philip supplemented visits to historic monuments with excursions to recent buildings. He saw the Bauhaus in Dessau after it had been converted by the Nazis to a training college, 'grumpily occupied by lady Gauleiters-in-training'. In Paris, he 'developed the habit of collecting specimens of the new white architecture of Le Corbusier'.[3] Travelling south, he went to visit the young artist (and family friend) Leonora Carrington (b.1917) in the house she shared with her lover, Max Ernst, near Avignon, and felt that 'things were really beginning to roll'. In Holland, he visited Van Tijen & Maaskant's Plaslaan housing in Rotterdam and other Dutch housing projects that certainly influenced his own work. In due course, the die was cast: Powell abandoned his Cambridge scholarship and went to the AA. When war broke out in 1939, the pacifist convictions which he maintained all his life meant that he would become a conscientious objector. Fortunately – for that decision embarrassed his family – he was rejected for service as unfit (his diminutive stature earned him the nickname 'Titch') and was able to continue his studies at the AA. His commitment to the Modern Movement was passionate. In 1942, he went with fellow student Geoffry Powell to see a house, 'Hill Pasture', at Broxted, Essex, designed by Ernö Goldfinger – that architect's first built work in Britain, completed in 1937. Powell was surprised, but then hugely impressed, that the house was not covered in white render but in something 'more subtle, more lasting – brickwork, in simple, bold areas of imperforate walls alternating with floor to ceiling windows'.[4] (Michael Powell was, in fact, working with Goldfinger at the time – part of the 'camouflage unit' operating from the latter's office in Bedford Square and also including such talents as Julian Trevelyan and Roland Penrose.)

Two views of the Powell & Moya office in 1955. Philip Powell and Hidalgo Moya. The gilt-framed David Cox oil hangs above a model of the Skylon.

Hidalgo 'Jacko' Moya was an American by birth, born at Los Gatos, California, on 5 May 1920, the son of a Mexican-born inventor, violin-maker and would-be entrepreneur (also Hidalgo – he died when Moya was just six) and an English mother. He was brought to England at the age of one, and later schooled at Oundle and at the Royal West of England College of Art in Bristol.

The drawing office on the top floor: left to right, John Cottwell, Bernard Throp, Robert Huddleston, Derek Stow, Michael Huckstepp.

Moya was initially drawn to engineering as a career, but his maths was 'a bit ropey' and he opted for architecture instead. He entered the AA in 1938. Moya was a man of many talents – hugely practical and inventive, like his father, and a notable artist who sketched constantly. Rejected, like Powell, for military service, Moya was a brilliant, if unpredictable, student, and was in tune with the radical thinking of the AA, where the social gospel of the Modern Movement was already firmly entrenched. Philip Powell remembered Moya as 'a brilliant yet unstudious student. If, on occasion, his term's work could not be properly acclaimed, it could be that the drawing machine he had invented, detailed and constructed was ready less than a day before the studio work for which it was intended had to be submitted.'[5] During the war years, the AA was evacuated to High Barnet, where the extension of the Northern Line had conveniently opened in 1940. Powell and Moya shared a house (christened 'Taliesin') with ten other students, each paying £1 a week in rent. Geoffry Powell, apparently unrelated to Philip but a firm friend and later a partner with Peter ('Joe') Chamberlin and Christof Bon in the practice of Chamberlin, Powell and Bon, was one of them. Jeannie Moya (Jacko Moya's second wife – they married in 1988) was another – 'he got me through the mechanics paper', she recalls – as was Michael Powell, before his call-up to the army.

Philip Powell – methodical, painstaking with clients and a witty public speaker – and Moya – intuitive, bohemian in manner and with no taste for business matters – formed a partnership that lasted until both retired from practice in the early 1990s. Their work together at the AA, where they collaborated with fellow student Margaret Taylor on a diploma scheme for housing in Bethnal Green, led to continued collaboration in the office of Frederick Gibberd (1908–84), Principal of the AA in succession to Geoffrey Jellicoe, during the war years. Already well-known as the architect of the strikingly modern, critically acclaimed Pullman Court flats in Streatham, completed in 1935, Gibberd went on to become the masterplanner of Harlow New Town, founder of one of the big post-war British practices and the architect of Gatwick Airport and Liverpool's Roman Catholic Cathedral. During the war years, he worked on the design of houses intended for mass production, using alternatives to conventional construction techniques, in response to a government programme. Gibberd's standard house, designed for the British Iron and Steel Federation, was one of a number of models constructed in considerable quantities – around 30,000 such houses had been completed by 1951. Gibberd also worked in association with the civil engineering contractors John Howard & Company, which established a design department in Datchet, Berkshire, under his supervision, recruiting Philip Powell and Jacko Moya as assistants, along with their fellow AA alumnus Geoffry Powell. The Howard House was the outcome. Designed to be erected either in the form of semi-detached pairs or in terraces, depending on the context, the Howard House was a progressive concept, eliminating brickwork and relying on 'dry' construction. The Howard system consisted of a series of prefabricated units mounted on a light steel frame of standard rolled sections. Site work was simply a matter of assembly – the frame could be erected in a matter of hours. The houses were roofed in asbestos sheets and externally clad in

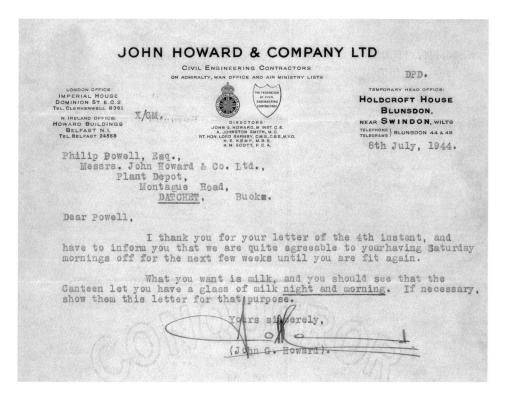

Letter to Powell from John G. Howard

insulated panels made of fibreboard, wood wool and aluminium foil. Services were concentrated in a prefabricated package, with bathrooms and kitchens backing on to each other at the end of the house.

Powell & Moya's involvement with the Howard House appears to have extended over much of 1944: both became employees of John Howard & Company for a time, though Moya continued to work from London. At this time, Powell's health was not good. In July, he requested, and was granted, the privilege of not working Saturday mornings until he was fit again. The firm's managing director, John G. Howard, wrote to him: 'What you want is milk, and you should see that the canteen let you have a glass of milk *night and morning.* If necessary, show them this letter for that purpose.'[6] In December, Philip Powell wrote to Howard signifying his intention to quit the firm's employment and giving the requisite one week's notice – 'I am about to start up in private practice,' he explained.[7] Howard subsequently asked Powell if he would consider continuing for a limited period on a part-time basis, three days per week, especially since Moya had agreed to accept a full-time appointment. Terms were agreed (£2 2s. per day, plus expenses) and one of Powell's tasks over the next month or so was to prepare material for an exhibition on 'The Post-War House' being organised at Dorland Hall in London by the *Daily Herald.* The working relationship with John Howard does not seem to have

Fitted kitchen in one of the Highworth houses

been a happy one, however: in April 1945, Powell wrote to him to complain that 'the architects, as such, are ignored and are used as mere draughtsmen. As I am particularly busy at the moment, I do not feel very much encouraged to give three days of my week to carry out work for which an architect does not seem to be required.'[8] Shortly after, it seems, Powell went his own way.

Philip Powell and Jacko Moya's involvement in the quest for the low-cost house, however, continued. The prototype 'pair of Highworth Houses', constructed in the small town of the same name near Swindon, were completed in 1951 and were widely published. Designed by the young partnership in association with Eric Chick, 'a Wiltshire builder, but also a sort of genius' as Powell described him, they appeared less radical than the Howard House, combining traditional and non-traditional materials and methods of construction. (A major objective was to economise on the use of steel, a costly material still in short supply after the war.) End walls, party walls and cross-walls were of brick, with remaining, non-loadbearing external walls constructed on a light-weight frame and other internal walls no more than partitions. Saving up to a quarter of the usual construction time, and with significant cost reductions (the quantity of bricks used was 60 per cent less than that for a conventional house), the concept was aimed at local authorities striving to meet government housing targets. A terrace of similar houses were subsequently built at Highworth and rented out at £2 per week, and 20 more were constructed at Baughurst, Hampshire, for Kingsclere Rural District Council. Thereafter, the programme appears to have stalled. For Reyner Banham, profiling Powell & Moya in 1974, the partnership of Chick and Powell & Moya had produced nothing less than the prototype of the British post-war house, far more significant than the Howard Houses and neither a lightweight prefab nor a solid brick structure of the sort built by the thousand between the wars. It was the model for Eric Lyons's Span housing and was taken up by 'practically every spec builder from Freshwater, Isle of

Highworth houses when new: the resident in the picture was still living there in 2008

Wight, northwards'. Indeed, 'it *is* the post-war British house … if the history of architecture had anything much to do with the facts of everyday building, the Highworth house would have by far the largest entry in the chapter on "Britain after 1950".[9] More than half a century on, the houses at Highworth were among the six winners of Diamond Jubilee awards in the Housing Design Awards, 2008. 'This unassuming terrace conceals a radical approach to planning and construction which was at least ten years ahead of its time,' declared the jury. One of the original residents, Mrs Pat Lay, now in her 80s, was found to be still living, very contentedly, in the house into which she and her late husband had moved in 1953, having brought up three children there.

For Powell & Moya, however, the task of building Churchill Gardens was the overwhelming priority at this time. In 1947, the young Peter Skinner joined the practice.

Mrs Pat Lay, one of the original Highworth residents

Skinner was a thoroughly practical type. Lacking a formal architectural education
– the RIBA later gave him an honorary fellowship – he had trained at Brixton School
of Building and worked for Deptford and Wandsworth councils as well as for Edwin
Lutyens's son, Robert. Skinner effectively took on the running of Powell & Moya's office:
the hiring and firing of staff, the supervision of the finances and the administration of
projects. His contribution to the realisation of Churchill Gardens was enormous. (In
1961 he became a partner in the practice along with Robert Henley (d.1973) and he
retired in 1986.) Derek Stow, who joined the firm in 1953 after National Service – he
had already done a stint with Chamberlin, Powell and Bon – remembers Philip Powell
as 'a great conceptualist – a typical AA product, full of ideas, but not enormously
concerned with the details'. Moya was 'even more of an ideas man', but with no interest
in the practical issues of running an office. When Skinner joined the firm, with its
offices in Great Smith Street, Westminster, there were just nine members of staff. 'There

Aerial view of Churchill Gardens

The first phase of Churchill Gardens consisted of four nine-storey blocks

is only as much work in the office as the two partners can give a personal creative direction to', reported *Architecture and Building* in 1955.[10] The ethos of the office, housed in rooms that were 'rather shabby, rather bare, candidly furnished with drawing boards and T squares', was informal, that of a creative atelier, and distinctly unhierarchical – this at a time when the partners of the typical practice were very much a breed apart from their assistants, usually closeted in private offices. At Powell & Moya, bottles of wine tended to be opened towards the end of the working day – 'there was always a drink to be had', Peter Skinner recalls. (Peter Dominic, soon to become a national name in the wine business, was a friend of Philip Powell and supplied wine at trade prices.) In due course, when post-war travel restrictions were eased, there were office jaunts: initially across the Channel to Boulogne and Le Touquet, later as far afield as Florence – 'they were very jovial outings', says Skinner.

Philip Powell, who married Philippa Eccles in 1953, had taken on the tenancy of a house in the Little Boltons, Kensington, in the late 1940s. The area was then far from fashionable and the house became the abode of a number of itinerant architects – including, for a time, Jacko Moya and Geoffry Powell – with something of the character of a student lodging house. Surviving residents from those years recall that it was cold and damp, with few conveniences – Jeannie Moya went down with pneumonia during one hard winter. In 1953, following his marriage, Powell was able to buy the house for £4,000, living there until he died in 2003. (Philippa Powell died three years later.) By this time, the Little Boltons had changed beyond recognition, with houses selling for millions of pounds, mostly to wealthy foreigners, and Number 16 stood out from its expensively restored neighbours, not least for the horizontal first-floor windows inserted by Powell at a time when conservation areas did not exist. Philip Powell's social and professional eminence notwithstanding, there was always an air of belated bohemianism at Number 16 – dinner parties there could be lively affairs and there was generally a bottle of champagne in the fridge, even if it was devoid of food. Jacko Moya, typically, eschewed a house in a convenient part of London. (He had married Jannifer Hall in 1947; the marriage broke down in the 1970s and was dissolved in 1985.) He opted instead for a converted barn in Epping Forest. The long Tube journey into central London, he said, gave him time to think: he would arrive at the office with a design in his head and immediately sit down and draw it up. Roger Burr, who joined Powell & Moya in 1969 and subsequently became a partner, recalls 'stories of his house in Epping Forest circulated at the time adding to his growing reputation – the room at the top of the house with a retractable stair and sliding glass walls, slabs of slate retrieved from the former public baths where the original Powell & Moya office in Great Smith Street was based, and horses that shared the freedom of the house'.

One of the nine-storey blocks seen from Churchill Square, with maisonette blocks completed in 1952

The accumulator tower at Churchill Gardens served Britain's first district heating scheme

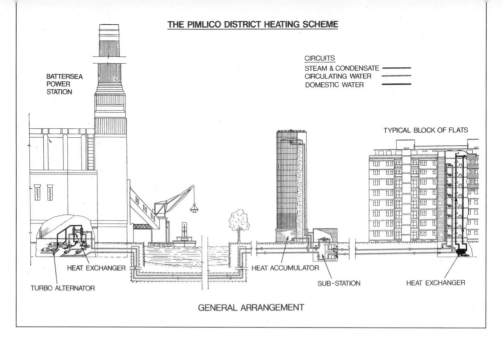

THE PIMLICO DISTRICT HEATING SCHEME

BATTERSEA
POWER
STATION

CIRCUITS
STEAM & CONDENSATE ————
CIRCULATING WATER ————
DOMESTIC WATER ————

TYPICAL BLOCK OF FLATS

HEAT EXCHANGER

TURBO ALTERNATOR

HEAT ACCUMULATOR

SUB-STATION

HEAT EXCHANGER

GENERAL ARRANGEMENT

Drawing of the Pimlico district heating scheme

Churchill
Gardens at night

One of the ten-storey blocks in the second phase of development at Churchill Gardens, complete with distinctive rooftop water tanks

The construction of Churchill Gardens began in 1948, following site clearance. The masterplan provided for a series of high-rise blocks standing at right angles to the river, with lower-rise blocks parallel with the Thames. The development was to be built in phases, the first element of phase 1 – completed in summer 1951 – consisting of 370 flats in a series of four nine-storey slab blocks (the maximum height then allowable) which were subsequently named after poets of the Romantic era. The flats were accessed by lifts and staircases, the latter expressed as glazed projections along one elevation while canted balconies enlivened the other facade. There were clear memories of the Dutch housing schemes that Philip Powell had seen and admired – not least in the use of yellow brick, as a cladding over the reinforced-concrete frame, on a plinth of blue engineering brick. This was a practical choice: the render used on many pre-war UK Modernist buildings had already weathered badly. The use of colour – sky blue, poppy red and grass green – on the rear walls of the balconies introduced a theme that was to persist in later phases of the development. A prominent – and, indeed, vital – feature of this first phase of construction was the accumulator tower, storing hot water channelled below the Thames from Battersea Power Station and used to service Britain's first ever district heating scheme. (Tenants were soon complaining that the heat was switched off at 10.00 p.m.) Clad with rough-cast glass in aluminium framing,

13

A staircase in Moyle House, part of the final phase of development at Churchill Gardens, completed in 1962

the 41-metre (136-foot) high tower was, and remains, a strikingly timeless structure, the design of which suggests the close involvement of Moya, working with assistant Martin Hurley. The block at the base of the tower, containing the pump house and workshops, is frankly Miesian, in the manner of the boiler house at IIT, with glazing set in black-painted steel framing exposing the machinery to public view.

In the second part of phase 1, completed in 1952, development pushed up towards the northern boundary of the site on Lupus Street, where a seven-storey block, De Quincey House, contained three tiers of two-storey maisonettes with shops at street level – a recognition of the need to provide the estate with the amenities of an established residential quarter. The shops, still thriving more than half a century later, are set back from the pavement under segmental arches. (In 1952, one of Britain's first 'self-service' stores opened there.) A second block to the east, virtually a replica, was built as part of the third development phase. Behind are six four-storey blocks of maisonettes, clad in rendered brickwork.

The second phase of development at Churchill Gardens (1951–4) took place on the western sector of the site and included blocks up to ten storeys high, strongly modelled and with the circular roof-top drums (containing water tanks) that became a distinctive feature of the project. In these blocks, balcony access replaced the earlier strategy of lifts and stairs serving just two flats per floor, partly because this later phase contained a greater number of smaller flats (of three rooms, or even fewer). In fact, since the LCC had relaxed its internal height requirements for dwelling spaces, these blocks were no higher than the nine-storey slabs in phase 1. Aesthetically, their boldly articulated facades provide a strong contrast to the latter, which had been condemned, even before they were completed, by the AA's student journal for their 'strangely out-moded appearance' which did not reflect 'the second Scandinavian invasion of the ateliers of this country and of the studios of Bedford Square'.[11] Even a few years after their graduation from the AA, Powell and Moya were, it seems, considered by some to be out of touch with leading-edge thinking.

The second phase of Churchill Gardens bears comparison with other high-density housing projects of the period, including the LCC's Loughborough Road estate in Lambeth, the first phase of the Alton Estate at Roehampton and Donald Gibson's flats at Tile Hill, Coventry – all completed in 1955–6. Phase 2 of Churchill Gardens also included low-rise housing facing the river along Grosvenor Road and intended to be let at 'economic' rents – that is, aimed at a more prosperous, potentially middle-class clientele. The inclusion of this element reflected the mood of a period in which the post-war housing programme had addressed the urgent needs of those displaced and made homeless as a result of the war, and, equally, the aim to create a socially mixed development rather than a working-class ghetto – the smaller flats also appealed to aspiring young professionals who might not yet have families.

Stage 3 of the project, including the second seven-storey block containing shops and a children's library on Lupus Street, was completed in 1959–60 and included two ten-storey blocks plus three-storey blocks of flats and maisonettes influenced by J. J. P. Oud's Kiefhoek estate in Rotterdam, which Powell had visited soon after the war. The fourth and final phase of the project was completed in 1962 on the eastern edge of the site, facing Claverton Street, and included a long block, clad in white tiles, spanning across the spine road of the estate. Earlier plans for tall slabs on this side of the site were abandoned, and the emphasis in this phase of development was on providing small flats aimed at the elderly.

In 2000, the Civic Trust celebrated the 40th anniversary of its annual awards scheme, resolving to give a special award to the project that had, in the view of the judges, done most for the cause of civilised, socially responsible development. The winner was Churchill Gardens. 'Churchill Gardens', the Trust proclaimed, 'demon-strates that high-density inner-city housing can be enduringly successful, a lesson that is more relevant than ever today.' The estate, it was noted, was highly popular with those living there – half the flats had been sold, mostly to former tenants under legis-lation introduced by Margaret Thatcher's government. It provided a heartening example of a post-war housing scheme that, in contrast to many others of the period, really worked. Not all the residents were so enthusiastic, and there were some complaints about the management of the estate by a private contractor. The press, however, generally applauded the decision. For Jonathan Glancey, writing in *The Guardian*, this 'handsome group of buildings' represented 'one way of building decent homes on a dense scale in city centres for people on average to low incomes without sacrificing light, air and dignity'.[12] Paul Finch, editor of the *Architectural Review* (*AR*), who grew up in Churchill Gardens, recalled a coherent community in which crime was almost unknown. 'Something of that generosity of spirit is attached to the estate,' Finch wrote, adding, 'to me it feels new, self-confident and optimistic'.[13]

Nearly 50 years earlier, the *AR* had commissioned the distinguished American critic and historian Henry-Russell Hitchcock to place Churchill Gardens in the context of new architecture internationally. Hitchcock was impressed by the accumulator tower and pump house ('if not quite a Miesian diamond, it is yet the finest bit of American paste in Britain') and by Powell & Moya's use of colour. However, his key focus was on the urbanistic aspects of the scheme. De Quincey House, with its shops, 'has something of the happy integration of the domestic and the commercial that exists in all old cities', he wrote. 'The ultimate success or failure of the Pimlico development as archi-tectonic urbanism remains uncertain,' he continued, adding, 'the promise of Pimlico is a multiple one ... what has already been accomplished is most encouraging, as is the evidence that the command by the architects of their problem has continually increased during the seven years they have been at work'.[14] The young Colin St John Wilson loved 'the impression of lightness and gaiety'.[15] Peter Shepheard, writing in *The Listener* in December 1950, found Churchill Gardens 'full not only of youthful enthusiasm, but also of a maturity, a balance, and a control of detail which make it an object lesson in housing'.[16] Like many subsequent commentators, Shepheard drew parallels between the development and the earlier housing schemes that created London's Georgian fabric. Another American critic, G. E. Kidder Smith, wrote that 'architecturally the buildings range from good to very good, although a too restless vocabulary of types rankles'.[17]

Nonetheless, Churchill Gardens did not receive universal critical acclaim. John Summerson, the great historian of Georgian London, writing in the *New Statesman*, found it 'foreign' in character, a late expression of Modernist thinking of the inter-war years. 'It does not arrive at what London so profoundly needs – a pattern of renewal which will be lived in because it is loved and not merely because there is nowhere else to live.'[18] Lewis Mumford found Churchill Gardens 'singularly depressing', commenting: 'It consists of great rows of nine-storey apartments, mostly grouped around the perimeter of a large block within which are three-, four- and seven-storey buildings ...

The Balmoral Castle pub was one of a number of existing buildings retained in the Churchill Gardens development

The close-up effect is grim even now, and it will become even grimmer.'[19] Ian Nairn, in a more balanced critique, argued that the 'good bits' of the scheme 'nowhere quite come together to make a piece'.[20] Reyner Banham, (who had worked as a labourer on Churchill Gardens as a young man) commented, perceptively, in 1974 that 'the later blocks of Churchill Gardens, done in 1954–8, now look exactly like routine council architecture of a decade later; until you stand close enough to be able to see the details, which are much too good for the mid-Sixties'.[21]

The success of Churchill Gardens as a place to live may have much to do with its location, within walking distance of Victoria and Sloane Square. The surrounding 19th-century housing, still seedy and largely multi-occupied while Churchill Gardens was being built, has since come up in the world and now commands high prices from discerning professionals. Young architects and designers, who would not dream of even stepping inside the adjacent overscaled Neo-Georgian Dolphin Square, have bought into Powell & Moya's scheme, which shares something of the cachet of the Brunswick Centre and Chamberlin, Powell and Bon's Golden Lane. Looking back on the project towards the end of his life, Philip Powell conceded that there were faults in the masterplan – 'too much road', for example. Purist critics did not warm to the pragmatism of the layout, with its mix of streets and open green space, but today the generosity of the planning is striking, a feature absent from many 'luxury' housing developments across London. Equally appealing, though a compromise in its own way, is the survival of older buildings within the estate – the Victorian school and church house belonging to St Gabriel's Church, for example, and the Balmoral Castle pub (long

The Gospel Oak housing included both high-rise and low-rise units, the latter with private gardens

closed and semi-derelict, sadly, in 2008) – though the 1870s Church of All Saints which stood on the riverside was demolished in the 1970s.

The greatest compliment that can be paid to the scheme is the fact that it seamlessly slots into the Victorian fabric of Pimlico. In its relationship to the city and its interplay of architecture and landscape, Churchill Gardens, a heroic achievement in its own right, prefigures much of Powell & Moya's subsequent work, including the much-admired Oxbridge housing projects. In an interesting postlude to Churchill Gardens, Philip Powell was assessor, in 1961, of a competition for the design of new housing for Westminster Council at Lillington Street, off Vauxhall Bridge Road – the role filled by Ramsey back in 1946. Powell & Moya had, in fact, been approached with a view to the practice taking on the job, and Philip Powell drew up a detailed masterplan showing how the site could respond to the competition brief, but they declined the commission on the grounds that the office was already overstretched with existing work. Out of over 150 submissions, including proposals by Barry Gasson, Ron Herron, and Bicknell and Hamilton, Powell selected that by John Darbourne, then aged 26, who subsequently formed the practice of Darbourne and Darke with Geoffrey Darke. The Lillington Gardens Estate, completed in stages between 1964 and 1972, is now listed.

Ian Nairn found Powell & Moya's housing at Lamble Street, Gospel Oak, altogether more convincing than Churchill Gardens. The latter, he argued, was 'not a real place'; this was. The Gospel Oak development, completed in 1954, consisted of one ten-storey

The Meadow Mews housing scheme in Lambeth includes an 18-storey tower, along with low-rise terraces

The central garden square is the most distinctive feature of Powell & Moya's housing scheme at Endell Street, Covent Garden

slab plus low-rise terraces, constructed on the lines of the Highworth Houses – 'proper houses, with proper back gardens that are a riot of rose-bushes after ten years. With the simplest of means, here is a real relationship, not an arrangement on paper.'[22] The client at Lamble Street was the St Pancras Borough Council. The scheme provided for 99 dwellings, half of them in the slab block, on a site which, extraordinarily, had never been developed, having been used as 'a junk yard and dumping ground'. The terraced houses had rear access to gardens 'in order that garden soil, manure, etc, need not be carried through the house'. A dramatic feature of the site, as found, was a spoil tip, 6 metres (20 feet) high, formed by the excavation of the nearby railway cutting. The tall block was placed on this mound, elevating it above the terraces. The architect John Winter, who has lived and worked in Camden for many years, recalled the 'mild dismay' that greeted the scheme: 'houses with gardens seemed reactionary in form and inappropriate in scale to the brave new London of popular imagination'.[23] The quality of Lamble Street, one of the first of a long series of innovative 'social' housing schemes in what became the London Borough of Camden, makes one regret that Powell & Moya did so little housing in the 50 years of the firm's existence. The housing projects that were realised, in the 1960s in south London for the Greater London Council and in Covent Garden in the early eighties, are, perhaps, not among the practice's major works.

The Meadow Mews project in Lambeth occupies a triangular site close to Kennington Oval, and recalls Lamble Street in combining a high-rise block with low-rise terraces. In this instance, however, the tall block extended to 18 storeys. The remainder of the housing, ranging in height from two to five storeys, featured enclosed yards rather than the verdant gardens of Gospel Oak. For all its large scale – nearly 300 dwelling units – the scheme received no publicity whatsoever. Did this reflect Powell's known distaste for tower-block housing?

Dudley Court in Endell Street, Covent Garden, was to be Powell & Moya's last housing project. The commission from Camden Council came to the practice in 1976; the scheme – built on the site of a demolished workhouse, later a factory, and with 90 flats and maisonettes, 23 of them sheltered accommodation for the elderly – was completed in 1983. It hardly reads as a typical work by the office. Its stock-brick-clad facades, combined with pitched, tile-clad roofs, appear to draw, rather half-heartedly, on the example of Lillington Gardens. The most positive aspect of the development is the generous open space at its heart – there were no private gardens. A day nursery, doctors' surgery, and laundry were also included in the scheme. Flats were accessed by open decks, leading to the charge that this was 'repro inter-war housing'. Colin Davies, reviewing the scheme in *Building Design*, was more generous, while considering it 'a curious hybrid' stylistically. 'Looked at one way, it is a straight modernist building one would expect from a practice that dates back to the Festival of Britain … It could be 1950s architecture, except for those bricks and tiles.' Covent Garden was, after all, 'a great place to live', though the rents were set at a level unaffordable by many locals. The range of amenities was, however, 'impressive'.[24] There was nothing here of the innovative thinking of Churchill Gardens and Lamble Street.

The house extension at Westgate, Chichester, the practice's first built work

Philip Powell's sister is seen sitting in the window of one of the houses at Mount Lane, Chichester

Interior of one of the Mount Lane houses, Chichester

The pair of houses at Oxshott, Surrey, included one house of two storeys and another on a single-storey plan

Alongside housing, there were houses by Powell & Moya – the earliest built in the context of severe restrictions on private residential development (no new dwelling could be larger than 465 square metres/15,000 square feet.) The first of these was not a new house but an extension, converted from an outhouse in the garden of a Georgian house in Chichester for an acquaintance of Philip Powell's father, who was by now installed in his canonry in the city. The converted building housed a one-bed flat. The two houses at Mount Lane, Chichester, followed. Canon Powell was facing retirement and the need to provide himself with a house for him and his wife Winifred after some years in Church properties. In addition, his daughter Joan had (in 1940) married Anthony Hogg, a naval officer and the son of a judge, whom she had met in Epsom. (Philip Powell, who was unused to strong drink, had got famously inebriated at the wedding reception and passed out on the bathroom floor. His father had to ascend a ladder and climb in through the bathroom window to rescue him.) The Hoggs, too, who now had a child, were in need of a house, and naval officers – like clergymen – were deemed 'key workers' and so able to bypass restrictions on 'inessential' building. In 1949, a former garden site around 0.4 hectares (1 acre) in extent, at Mount Lane, close to the heart of the city and within sight of the medieval cathedral, came up for sale and was acquired. The two houses were completed during the following year. Although new houses were restricted in terms of their size, the matter of cost was left to local authorities – the Mount Lane houses cost roughly the same as the new council houses then being built in Chichester. Carefully disposed in relation to each other and designed to make

Two views inside House I at Oxshott which
featured a combined kitchen and living area, a
progressive feature for the 1950s

minimum impact on the site and not to appear above the enclosing garden wall, they were modest structures, flat-roofed and externally rendered, with some use of colour. Inside both houses, antique furniture fitted comfortably into the austere modern interiors. Sadly, following the deaths of the original residents, one of the houses has been demolished and the other stands semi-derelict (2008).

The pair of houses designed by Powell & Moya at Oxshott, Surrey, completed in 1954, were commissioned by two civil servants, Howell Leadbeater and Desmond Keeling, who split the sloping, triangular 1.6-hectare (4-acre) site between them. Leadbeater wanted a single-storey house, Keeling a two-storey residence. Widely published, the two houses, costing around £4,000 each, were designed to form a group but to address the individual needs and tastes of the two clients, one of whom had three children. Long and thin in plan and clad in London stock brick, they took maximum advantage of the excellent views out to the south, with living rooms and bedrooms along the southern elevation, and were terraced down the sloping site, so that House 2, built for the Keelings and christened 'Headlong Hill', terminated in a two-storey wing. In tune with progressive thinking (by early fifties middle-class standards), House 1

The house at Leamington Spa, designed for Moya's mother, was demolished in the 1980s

Powell & Moya's finest private house, occupies a dramatic site at Toy's Hill in Kent

The Toy's Hill house takes maximum advantage of views from the fine hillside site

('Milk Wood') featured a single, combined living and dining space serviced by a long, thin, highly functional kitchen. Furnishings were generally contemporary designs. Each house cost around £1,400. Ian Nairn, writing in *The Buildings of England: Surrey*, found them 'very fine … Flat roofs, stock-brick walls and deep white-painted eaves, a spare industrial style which only Powell & Moya in England at this date managed to humanize'.[25] The dwellings survive, but have been spoiled by ill-conceived alterations.

The house designed for Jacko Moya's widowed mother on a garden site at Leamington Spa and completed in 1956 has suffered a worse fate: complete demolition in the 1980s. It was a long, low structure in the mould of the Chichester houses, but with a leanness of detail that suggests the influence of Mies, and was never adequately published or recorded. In this light, the survival of Powell & Moya's most ambitious private house at Toy's Hill, near Westerham, Kent, is all the more welcome. It was built for two spinster sisters, Monica and Muriel Anthony, as a weekend retreat from London. The women had inherited a house nearby from their parents. It was sold, but some land was retained for a new dwelling. Ian McCallum of the *AR*, a friend of Monica, recommended Powell & Moya for the job. The site was splendid, commanding a fine view of the Weald. As at Oxshott, it sloped markedly, falling away from the road which provided the means of access, so it was decided to place the garage, plus a useful box room, at first-floor (road) level, with the house extending out along the flatter ground below. 'The route from garage to bedrooms is downhill all the way, which is no doubt comforting for the owners when they arrive, weary and luggage-laden, for the weekend,' commented *Country Life*. The plan gave most of the rooms the advantage of excellent views out to the south. A central hallway cut the house effectively in half, with living room, dining room and kitchen to the west and the three bedrooms and bathroom on a slightly lower level to the east. It was the nature of the site, in part, that generated the elements of drama in the architecture. *Country Life* reported that 'so dynamic is the appearance of the house that it has almost defeated its primary purpose, as the owners' privacy is frequently disturbed at weekends by unsolicited visits from enthusiastic students of contemporary architecture'.[26]

Inevitably, Churchill Gardens dominated the early years of the practice, with Philip Powell closely involved with the development, though there were soon other projects to grapple with: the Festival of Britain Skylon, still Powell & Moya's most famous project; the first of very many hospital jobs; and, in 1957, the commission for a new building at Brasenose College, Oxford, the first of a series of additions to Oxbridge colleges. Hospitals and educational buildings were to become the core of Powell & Moya's workload in the decades to come, but with Churchill Gardens the practice had changed the face of London and made a dramatic statement about the potential for renewing Britain's tired and war-ravaged cities.

Notes

1   Philip Powell, 'Adventure with caution', *Civic Focus*, Spring 2000, p11.
2   ibid.
3   Philip Powell, 'A wartime visit to Hill Pasture', *DoCoMoMo UK Newsletter,* 8, Summer 1996, p5.
4   ibid.
5   Obituary of Moya, *Architects' Journal,* 11 August 1994, p8.
6   Typescript letter in Powell & Moya archive.
7   Draft letter in Powell & Moya archive.
8   Powell & Moya archive.
9   Reyner Banham, 'Nice, modern and British!', *New Society,* 18 July 1974, p161. For a technical account, see 'Low cost houses at Highworth', *Architecture and Building News*, 15 November 1951, pp542–9.
10 *Architecture and Building News*, August 1955, p305.
11 *Plan,* 1, 1948, p19.
12 Jonathan Glancey, 'Village idiots', *The Guardian*, 3 April 2000.
13 *The Independent*, 13 February 2000.
14 Henry-Russell Hitchcock, 'Pimlico', *Architectural Review*, September 1953, pp177–84.
15 Colin St John Wilson, 'Patterns in living', *The Observer*, 20 July 1952.
16 Peter Shepheard, 'Young architects' triumph in Pimlico', *The Listener*, 21 December 1950, p777.
17 G. E. Kidder Smith, *The New Architecture of Europe* (London, 1961), p44.
18 John Summerson, 'A Piece of New London', *New Statesman and Nation*, 29 December 1951, p755.
19 Lewis Mumford, 'London can teach us', *New Yorker*, 18 October 1953. See also Frank Jessup, Wolfson College, Oxford, A Short History (new edn, Oxford, 1999).
20 Ian Nairn, *Modern Buildings in London* (London, 1964), p17.
21 Banham, op. cit., p161.
22 Ian Nairn, *Nairn's London* (Harmondsworth, 1966), p211.
23 John Winter, 'Modern homes in Camden', *RIBA London Region Yearbook*, 1984, p95.
24 Colin Davies, 'Housing Hybrid', *Building Design*, 15 April 1983, pp30–1.
25 Ian Nairn and Nikolaus Pevsner, *The Buildings of England, Surrey* (2nd edn, Harmondsworth, 1971), p401. See also *Architecture and Building News*, 15 December 1955, pp769–75.
26 H. Dalton Clifford, 'A house that surveys the Weald', *Country Life*, 7 August 1958, p287.

CHAPTER TWO:
1951 and the Skylon

The 1951 Festival of Britain was famously conceived as 'a tonic for the nation' – a Britain worn down by six years of war following a long period of recession, and still contending with severe economic problems, including the rationing of food and most of the other things that made life bearable. Gerald Barry, who became Director-General of the Festival (and was, coincidentally, the stepfather of architect Richard Burton), had been campaigning for some time for an event to be held in 1951 to mark the centenary of the Great Exhibition of 1851. The original idea was for an international trade exhibition which would promote the cause of British industry and design, much as the 1851 Exhibition had done. The trade fair idea, however, quickly evaporated, while the Labour government eagerly took up the idea of an exhibition that would simply celebrate British achievements – 'a national display illustrating the British contribution to civilization, past, present and future, in arts, in science and technology, and in industrial design', as the prominent Cabinet member (and minister in charge of the Festival) Herbert Morrison put it. One of the great ironies of the project was that by the time the Festival opened (in May 1951) the optimism generated in many by the Labour election victory of 1945 had largely evaporated. The Labour government was in disarray, rent by divisions, its majority slashed in an election the previous year. Britain was again at war – in Korea. Meat rations were cut, coal was in short supply and, on top of everything, the spring of 1951 was exceptionally cold and wet. The closure of the Festival in September 1951 was followed by another election, which saw Labour ejected from power (for 13 years, as it turned out) and Winston Churchill back in 10 Downing Street. For many politically and socially idealistic architects of the younger generation, including Jacko Moya and Philip Powell, this turn of events must have been extremely depressing (though the 'Butskellite' consensus between Labour and the Conservatives that dominated British politics into the 1970s ensured that the Welfare State was not dismantled).

It was clear from the first that, in architectural and design terms, the Festival would be a celebration of the new and innovative. Hugh Casson, whom Barry appointed as its Director of Architecture, saw it as an opportunity for the great reservoir of creativity held back by the years of war and austerity to be unleashed – here was scope for 'everyone's pent-up fifth-year scheme' to be realised. The architectural team appointed by Casson to build a total of nearly 33,000 square metres (350,000 square feet) of buildings on the 11-hectare (27-acre) South Bank site included Ralph Tubbs (the Dome

Opposite: Skylon by night, a potent symbol of the festival of Britain

of Discovery), H. T. ('Jim') Cadbury-Brown (the Concourse, the Land of Britain and the People of Britain), Brian O'Rorke (Country Pavilion), Basil Spence (Sea and Ships Pavilion), Eric Brown and Peter Chamberlin (Seaside Pavilion) and Jane Drew (Riverside Restaurant). Smaller commissions went to, among others, Wells Coates and Edward Mills. The mix of relatively untried younger talents and established names with built work dating back to the inter-war years (for example, Wells Coates and Basil Spence) was judicious. Equally pragmatic was the decision to commission most of the buildings by direct appointment. Only two were open to competition. That for a restaurant and bar was won by the young Leonard Manasseh. The competition (with a premium of £300) for a 'vertical feature', a structure without a practical function which could be 'completely abstract in conception or related to the theme of the exhibition' and was budgeted at £14,000, attracted 157 entries, some of them from artists such as Duncan

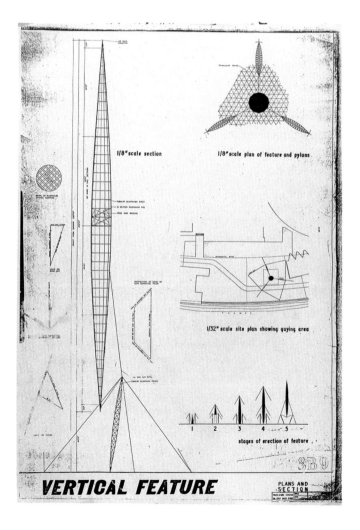

A drawing illustrating the phases of construction for the Skylon, the key feature of the 1951 Festival of Britain

The Skylon stood close to the river Thames and to Ralph Tubb's Dome of Discovery

Grant and Quentin Bell, and was won by Powell & Moya in January 1950, with their proposal for what became the Skylon.

As Philip Powell recalled many years later, 'Jacko and I did separate entries. I did a pyramid, a slightly tapering thing, with a zigzag bracing and a coloured pattern, but Jacko's first sketch felt so right that there was no point going further and we collaborated after that. But it was Jacko who evolved the design.'[1] Moya, assisted for a time by the young James Gowan, worked on the designs in collaboration with the engineer Felix Samuely, who had taught both Powell and Moya during their time at the AA – they had wanted him as engineer for Churchill Gardens, but had been overruled by the client in favour of Scott & Wilson. Austrian-born Samuely (1902–58) had already played a major role in the rise of modern architecture in Britain, collaborating with Connell, Ward and Lucas; Denys Lasdun; Berthold Lubetkin (as assistant to Ove Arup on the Penguin Pool); and Mendelsohn and Chermayeff (he was structural engineer for the De La Warr Pavilion, Bexhill).

The Skylon was conceived as a hollow 12-sided metal structure (actually constructed of a mix of steel and aluminium), 76 metres (250 feet) tall (not counting its base) and tapering to a point at top and bottom. Moya's initial idea had been for an inflatable structure – and there is perhaps just a hint of the Zeppelin in the shape, though the press variously compared it to a cigar, pencil or torpedo. By night, the structure would be illuminated by banks of lights within, changing in colour along its length. Moya, ever the engineer manqué, imagined the Skylon 'floating' like a balloon above the ground, which it would not appear to actually touch. (A *Punch* cartoon depicted Clement Attlee and Herbert Morrison gazing wistfully at the Skylon which, like their sinking government, had 'no visible means of support'.) It would be raised above the ground on a system consisting of three pylons with a cradle of steel cables. It was emphatically not to be a conventional tower.

Powell & Moya had submitted their competition design without consulting an engineer as to its practicality; Samuely was surprised to be asked to work on a scheme that had already been designed, but said he would see what could be done. Moya recalled the extent of his contribution:

> after a short while he got rid of six secondary cables which we had thought were necessary to stabilize the three pylons, and he reduced by half the tendency of the main body to sway in the wind, a well known wrecker of tall or thin structures. (As students we had watched with fascination the film of the collapse of the Tacoma Narrows bridge.) Samuely also intro-duced us to the idea of using the main supporting cables in compression as well as in tension, so that they acted like long and very thin struts. All this was done by tensioning the whole structure after it was assembled. Three hydraulic jacks, one under each pylon, were used to induce the tension … At the bottom of the cigar, the thin point where some of the greatest stresses occurred, Samuely managed to remove our rather bulky cable connectors by the simple but brilliant scheme of using continuous twin cables looped under shoes or cleats.

Samuely, Moya said, had transformed the Skylon 'into something so simple and clean looking that it seemed quite remarkable that it could remain standing'.[2]

Work on constructing – or, rather, assembling – the Skylon began in the summer of 1950. The main steel-lattice structure was fabricated in the factory of Painter Bros at Hereford, with the cladding of aluminium louvres made by F. Braby & Co. of Bristol. The process of erecting the Skylon was undertaken by a small, skilled and fearless team from British Insulated Callenders Cables – modern health-and-safety require-ments would have made the process considerably more protracted, and certainly much more costly. By March 1951, the Skylon was effectively complete and Philip Powell and Jacko Moya were hauled to the top in a basket, along with BBC commentator Wynford Vaughan Thomas, who broadcast from the basket. 'For the first time we had some idea of the skill of the men who built this structure working in such difficult and dangerous conditions,' Moya later recalled.[3] By the beginning of April, it was ready to 'beckon the world to Britain's greatest show in history', as an enthusiastic journalist commented.

The Skylon in course of erection in early 1951

Despite the sceptical comments of conservative critics – who tended to loathe the entire Festival – the Skylon captured the public imagination. It had become the 'Skylon' as the result of a competition in which members of the public were invited to suggest a name for the 'vertical feature'. The competition was won by Mrs Margaret Sheppard Fidler, whose husband was an architect (in fact, chief architect to Crawley New Town). 'We toyed with words like Skyhook and Pylon,' Mrs Fidler recalled, 'and, of course, visualized it in the London sky. Suddenly it seemed that "Skylon" would be a good name for this beautiful and exciting adornment of the London sky.' Philip Powell remembered that 'nylon was the great new invention, and the name seemed to fit the mood of the times'.[4] As the time came for the Festival to open, the widespread mood of scepticism – could Britain afford it? – became muted, and most Britons decided to enjoy the carnival.

'No visible means of support': this Punch cartoon compared the structure of the Skylon to the state of Britain and the declining Labour government

The Skylon received a generally positive press. The *New Statesman* captured the essence of the project: the structure had no function, and no obvious symbolism: 'it's like everything else in the Festival – a huge, lively joke, a tribute only to the spirit of nonsense and creative laughter. It may or may not earn dollars. Who cares? ... The Skylon is a cone of light in a dark world.'[5] *The Times* commented that 'the Skylon, whether it survives or not, will probably be one of the best remembered things of the exhibition'.[6] The veteran Neoclassicist architect, and sometime head of the Bartlett School at University College London, Sir Albert Richardson, was one of the few dissenting voices, fulminating that 'in the old days of decency a jet of water, an obelisk or a tall bronze mast would have been thought suitable. Present day theories incline to synthetic imitations of stratospheric rockets. Or what is even more unsatisfactory, a Heath Robinson erection which challenges the law of gravitation.'[7] John Summerson, who never warmed to Powell & Moya's work, dismissed the Skylon as 'a silly toy, a pretty toy and a dangerous one'. The public in general had no reservations – 8.5 million people came to the South Bank, sometimes as many as 100,000 of them in one day. And it was the Skylon, more than anything else on the site, that most of them remembered. There were Skylon chocolate biscuits, Skylon ties and a Skylon biro pen (then a costly novelty at 25 shillings). Asked whether the practice had received any royalties from the manufacturers of these objects, Moya replied: 'No, we got one free pen'.

The Skylon on its
riverside site

The Festival had never been intended to continue after 1951 and the structures,
with the exception of the Royal Festival Hall, were not built to last. Nonetheless, many
detected an element of spite in the alacrity with which the incoming Conservative
government ordered the clearance of the site. The Skylon, more than most of the
Festival structures, had potential for relocating elsewhere. The site of the Crystal Palace
at Sydenham was one suggested location. It was reported that Morecambe Council
wanted to buy the Skylon and erect it on their seafront. The holiday camp magnate Billy
Butlin considered putting it up as a feature of his one of his establishments, probably at
Filey or Pwllheli. The Marquess of Bath was interested in setting it up in the grounds

of his mansion at Longleat – an idea that appealed to Moya. In the event, none of these proposals came to anything. The Skylon was simply sold for scrap – suggestions that it had been carefully dismantled and stored were proved to be mistaken.

Even long after its destruction, the Skylon continued to be a popular icon. Interest in the Festival had been rekindled by events marking its 25th anniversary in 1976, including an exhibition at the Victoria and Albert Museum. Further events marked the 40th anniversary in 1991 – a few years earlier, a masterplan by Terry Farrell for the development of the South Bank Arts Centre had included provision for the possible re-erection of the Skylon and a subsequent masterplan by Richard Rogers (who remembered the huge impact the structure had on him when he visited the Festival as a young man) included the same provision. Further interest was generated by a television programme made by Dan Cruickshank and shown in 1994, by chance within days of Jacko Moya's death. The campaign to rebuild the Skylon continues.

Powell & Moya was involved with one other project linked to the 1951 Festival. The Newton-Einstein house was proposed for the site opposite the V&A in South Kensington, where Lutyens had proposed to erect a National Theatre – it is now occupied by Casson Conder's Ismaili Centre. In essence, the structure (never realised) consisted of a bowl 24 metres (80 feet) in diameter that would revolve at a speed of 50 km (30 miles) per hour.

> The shape of the bowl was to be such that persons standing on opposite sides would be at right angles to each other. The illusions created by such a revolving bowl would have been many and intriguing: cyclists passing each other in opposite directions would, at the right speed, be at right angles to each other in the vertical plane; a ball thrown at the right velocity could have been caught on the opposite side by the person who threw it; persons walking across the axis would have had to counteract a side thrust. The bowl was to be reached by entering a lift at ground level which was revolved to the speed of the bowl and raised to the floor below it. Access to the bowl from the floor was by staircase.

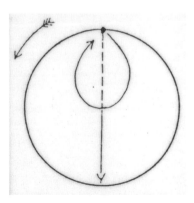

'It was a bit like a giant fairground ride,' Philip Powell admitted; 'in fact, Jacko and I were both made to go on the new ride [The Rotor] at Battersea Park under tarpaulin. We were both sick. That was the difference – it was alright if you could see.'[8]

The commission for the Chichester Festival Theatre came to Powell & Moya in 1958. Philip Powell's family connections with the cathedral city were obviously a significant factor. Canon Arnold Powell was still living there. His first wife,

Line drawing showing the principles behind Powell & Moya's proposed Newton-Einstein house.

Section drawing of the unrealised
Newton-Einstein house project,
designed for a site in South
Kensington

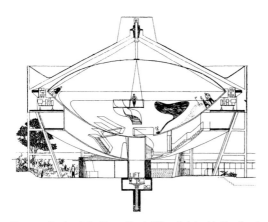

Above, a section through the Newton-Einstein " house," designed by Powell **and** *Moya, for the Festival of Britain, but never built. This building was intriguing in that it was meant to show the results arising from the conflict between the force of gravity and centrifugal forces. It was to consist of a bowl 80 ft. in diameter revolving at a perimeter speed of 30 m.p.h. The shape of the bowl was to be such that persons standing on opposite sides would be at right angles to each other. The illusions created by such a revolving bowl would have been many and intriguing ; cyclists passing each other in opposite directions would, at the right speed, be at right angles to each other in the vertical plane ; a ball thrown at the right velocity could have been caught on the other side by the person who threw it ; persons walking across the axis would have had to counteract a side-thrust. The bowl was to be reached by first entering a lift at ground level which was revolved to the speed of the bowl and raised to a floor below it. Access to the bowl from the floor was by staircase.*

Winnie, Philip's mother, had died in 1957 and he soon married again – the widow of a fellow canon.

The idea of the theatre was conceived by a local optician, councillor and friend of Arnold Powell, Leslie Evershed-Martin, who had been enthused by a television programme about the theatre founded by director Sir Tyrone Guthrie in Stratford, Ontario. Evershed-Martin resolved to establish a theatre in Chichester and contacted the biggest name on the British theatrical scene, Sir Laurence Olivier. In due course, Olivier agreed to become the theatre's artistic director – a considerable coup for Chichester. Evershed-Martin had the idea of the theatre as 'a tent in the park', housing a Glyndebourne-like summer festival which would attract the best in theatrical talent. He set about raising the funding needed (the final cost was £105,000) through voluntary donations. A site was secured – flat parkland close to the centre of the city. Powell & Moya were approached to design the building, but initially declined the job – being eventually persuaded to take it on. Derek Stow recalls Olivier visiting the practice office. 'He would arrive in a pale blue Rolls-Royce, dressed in an exquisitely tailored pale blue suit and bellow – "I want to see Powell". He wouldn't settle for anyone else in the office.' The job architect for the theatre was Christopher Stevens, who later worked for James Stirling. Bernard Throp, who joined the practice in 1957, also worked on the project.

The Chichester Festival Theatre auditorium was the first professional theatre in Britain to feature seating for audiences on three sides of the stage

The evolution of the design reflected the influence of Tyrone Guthrie, a passionate advocate of 'theatre in the round'. Olivier, like Evershed-Martin, was rather sceptical – 'I always felt that the open stage boys had gone back in time,' he admitted. Yet the experience of Chichester was crucial when Olivier began to plan the new National Theatre to be built on London's South Bank. The design of the latter's main auditorium (the Olivier) drew heavily on the lessons learned at Chichester. Philip Powell, it seems, did not warm to Olivier, and when the latter suggested that Powell & Moya might undertake the National Theatre job he declined, leaving the way open for Denys Lasdun to create his masterpiece.

The Chichester Festival Theatre was completed in time for the summer season in 1962. It is now listed Grade II*. The thrust stage was the feature that attracted attention: it was the first large theatre in Britain in which the audience was seated on three sides of the stage. The brief was for around 1,400 seats. Backstage facilities were to be minimal – 'a temporary hut will house the restaurant and the main workshop is a disused pub', reported the *Architects' Journal* (*AJ*). The absence of any backstage storage for scenery was a clear drawback. The 'tent in a park' idea led the architects to consider literally creating a tent, with a fabric roof – fire regulations quickly ruled out that idea. Instead, the roof was supported on cables bearing against the concrete ring beam circling the hexagonal auditorium, and supported on a ring girder of steel tubing resting on the cables – a structural strategy evolved by Charles Weiss & Partners, Powell & Moya's usual engineering consultants. The auditorium was entirely column-free – with seats, in four tiers, no more than 18 metres (60 feet) from the stage – and raised at first-floor level, with foyer, bar, cloakrooms and dressing rooms squeezed beneath. 'The virtues of this theatre are clear for all to see,' declared the *AJ*. 'It is an astonishing achievement for the cost and is certainly one of the most exciting and unusual buildings to be put up for a long time. It is challenging both in its demands on actors and audience and in its frank architectural character.'[9]

More than a decade after the opening of the theatre, some of its more obvious failings were addressed – with extensions to the existing envelope in order to contain an expanded box office, a larger bar area and, most importantly, improved backstage facilities, including vastly improved dressing rooms. Air-conditioning was installed in the auditorium (where the heat in the summer season had, on occasions, been unbearable). Something of the purity of the original concept was lost, but the theatre became a more enjoyable place for audiences, staff and actors. Critic Michael Webb considered Chichester 'a brilliant achievement: a theatre that offers English audiences and actors a revolutionary new environment at a cost within reach of voluntary contributions'.[10] As a venue, the theatre thrived, with an average 90 per cent attendance (1971) and a mailing list of 20,000 despite doubts as to whether Chichester could support an institution of this kind. Today, it acts as a producing house in the summer months and a receiving house in the winter. It is the straightforwardness, rigour and economy of the design that still

Chichester Festival Theatre exterior

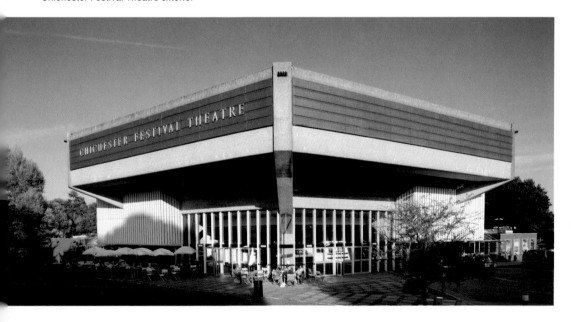

impresses – the bush-hammered concrete structure provides a striking modern intervention into a historic context. A year later, Peter Moro's Nottingham Playhouse opened
– a sophisticated and beautiful building that has aged well. The Playhouse, however, had
roughly half the seating capacity of Chichester – and cost twice as much. Like Mayfield
School some years before, the Chichester Festival Theatre was so cheap that only close
study of the figures convinced many that the reported budget was correct.

Mayfield School, completed in 1956, was followed, more than a decade later, by
another public commission in the near vicinity. The public baths at Putney, opened in
1968, had to be slotted into a tight corner site surrounded by houses. The architects
broke down the elements in the complex – including a training pool, L-shaped main
pool (with separate diving area) and public hall – to form an open-sided quadrangle
containing existing mature trees that were carefully retained. The lively external
elevation of the main pool reflected the dramatic form of the interior, with an exhilar-
ating roof structure engineered by Charles Weiss using long-span concrete V-beams.
What might, in other hands, have become a bulky interloper into the suburban scene
emerged as a friendly addition to the context, cleverly weaving the new buildings into
the mature landscape.

The commission to design the UK Pavilion for the Osaka Expo of 1970 came to
Powell & Moya in 1967. Suggestions that there should be an architectural competition were ignored by the Central Office of Information (COI), which was in charge of
the British contribution. The President of the RIBA was asked to shortlist six possible
practices and from this list Powell & Moya was selected, even though, apart from
the Skylon, the practice had never designed an exhibition building. Great international exhibitions became a regular event in the post-war decades. Brussels in 1958
was followed nine years later by Expo 67 in Montreal. The British Pavilion there was
designed by Basil Spence, then at the height of his success as the British Establishment's
'official' architect. Though relatively conventional when compared with the United
States Pavilion, by Buckminster Fuller, and Frei Otto's West German Pavilion, it was
generally judged a considerable success – the internal displays were coordinated by
James Gardner, who had worked on the Festival of Britain. With Osaka in the bag,
Philip Powell, Jacko Moya, Peter Skinner and Bob Henley rushed off to Expo 67, then in
its last days, to study the pavilions there. According to Moya, 'the first day was splendid,
everywhere exciting, amazing structures … After a couple of days amazement ceased.
It was tiring. It was a blooming mess. One longed for something plain, simple and flat.'[11]
Moya liked the Venezuelan Pavilion (by Carlos Raul Villanueva) for its simplicity and
air of calm, and the Frei Otto pavilion for its lack of regimentation.

The 1970 UK Pavilion had to fit into a masterplan by Kenzo Tange. A site was
chosen close to the western entrance into the Expo site. The brief from Ted Swaine of
the COI was quite precise: to provide space for four separate displays – 'Progress for
Mankind', 'the British Scene', 'British Heritage' and 'Building for the Future' – which
would be shown in artificially lit spaces. It was reckoned that up to 30,000 people a
day would visit the building – in fact, on the first Saturday of opening more than twice

that number crammed in. The overall budget for the pavilion was to be £2.5 million, of which the building itself should cost no more than £800,000. Moya, who headed the design team with Bob Henley and with Charles Weiss & Partners as structural engineers, found the prescriptive nature of the brief irksome. The demand for spaces without natural light 'seemed to remove any possibility of having a building where the inside and outside were designed as one'. Moreover, since the design of the building and the displays it was to house were not coordinated, the size and configuration of the internal spaces were unknown. There was also the certainty, given the requisite fixed route through the displays, that there would be queues of people to get in, getting either baked by the sun or drenched by the heavy rain that is a common feature of Japanese summers. Moya's solution was to turn the pavilion into a giant umbrella with a covered ground level, including areas of water, where people could queue for admission. The display spaces were above: four square boxes hung from a masted roof structure, accessed by ramps and stairs – the client ruled out the use of escalators. The roofline of the building was fixed, but there was scope for the size of the 'boxes' to vary. Far more than the 1967 Expo, that in 1970 was a shop window for radical architectural ideas – 'the most exhibitionist Expo ever', as Robin Boyd described it in a special issue

The interior of Putney Baths

of the *Architectural Review* (*AR*).[12] The experimental British combo of Archigram was given space in the central Festival Plaza; cables, masts and inflatable structures abounded. Frei Otto's 1967 pavilion had used masts to support a lightweight fabric roof – a strategy Otto was to use with even more spectacular effect in his 1972 Munich Olympics stadium. Powell & Moya's approach to the use of four masts, 33 metres (108 feet) high, supporting a 2-metre (6½-foot) deep diagrid roof – the initial idea was for a single mast – had more in common with the approach of the British high-tech architects of the 1970s and 80s, most obviously that of Nicholas Grimshaw.

Alongside some of the other pavilions, Britain's must have seemed relatively sober – what might Archigram or Cedric Price have made of it? Moya's instincts were to attempt something more radical than what was eventually built, but neither the brief nor the budget favoured experimentation. In fact, though it was not Moya's intention – 'it just turned out that way', he told the *AJ* – the pavilion had something of a Japanese flavour, thanks to its white panelled walls (of plywood, aluminium-faced, with 'Great Britain' spelled out in giant Japanese characters) and masts which had an echo of the monumental gates attached to traditional Japanese temples. The pavilion's national identity was further proclaimed by a Union Jack balloon anchored over it and, almost an afterthought, the painting of a huge version of the flag on its flat roof.

Moya saw the pavilion as 'a great big shed', an economical container for exhibits. The same agenda, many years later, drove Richard Rogers Partnership's designs – again

The open ground floor of the UK Pavilion at the 1970 Osaka Expo provided shelter for queuing visitors

Night view of the Osaka Expo Pavilion, showing the structural masts that prefigured later high-tech buildings

using a masted structure – for London's Millennium Dome. In both instances, however, there was a marked disjunction between the container and the contents. At Osaka, few were impressed by the latter despite the involvement of such respected designers as Casson Conder, Gordon Bowyer and Leslie Gooday. The blacked-out interiors were not enjoyable – the publication *Building* reported that visitors were forced to

> shuffle at a high rate of knots in a relentlessly moving stream through
> several hundred feet of dim walkways, subjected for most of the time to
> bursts of electronic sounds and cinema projections … the dazed, uncom-
> prehending foreign visitor staggers from this exposition of the British way
> of life having learned – what? … the impression that our designers are too
> clever by half and that British-made carpets scuff badly in wear.[13]

'Nobody stops to watch through the extended sequence of Churchill, Magna Carta, Habeas Corpus and Suffragettes,' opined the *AJ*.[14] Much of the internal space was not even used. Alongside the US Pavilion, which made good use of natural light internally, the *AJ* commented that the displays in the British Pavilion looked 'unimaginative and second-rate', though the pavilion itself was 'a building of outstanding quality', completed on schedule and on budget – and a very modest budget at that. But the fact that building and contents had been designed without any coordination between

Aerial view of the British Pavilion, Expo 70, Osaka, seen prior to opening

the two produced disastrous results. Even the idea of the 'umbrella' turned sour. 'The Japanese at Expo barge and shove in a fashion unknown in Britain,' reported the *AJ*.[15] First rope barriers then steel crush barriers, along with turnstiles, were installed, compromising the covered space.

There were clearly lessons to be learned at government level from the Expo 70 experience. However, Powell & Moya's pavilion had been almost universally well received (though relatively few Britons got to Osaka) and gave the practice a bounce at the start of a new decade. The 1970s saw it receive the Royal Gold Medal for Architecture (in 1974), with Philip Powell getting his knighthood in 1975. (He had been appointed OBE in 1957, Moya CBE in 1966.) It was not to be an easy decade for any architectural practice – jobs dried up and practices shed staff – but Powell & Moya more than survived, largely on the basis of its extensive hospital portfolio. Nonetheless, there were major disappointments. The projects for new British embassies in Bonn and Tokyo (the latter described by John Haworth, who joined the firm in 1975, as 'a gem of a project') remained unbuilt. Bob Henley, whose contribution to the Osaka project was very considerable, sadly died in 1973. Three years later, Bernard Throp and John Cantwell were brought in as partners alongside Powell, Moya and Skinner.

The Expo 70 Pavilion certainly exemplified Moya's preferred approach to design. Jack Pringle, who first went to Powell & Moya on his year out in 1972–3 and returned as a qualified architect in 1975, remembers Moya as 'a passionate technophile – he would as happily read *New Scientist* as *AJ*'. Moya, he says, 'greatly respected the new high-tech generation, especially Richard Rogers. The Pompidou Centre was a building that he hugely admired.' Reyner Banham saw the Expo 70 Pavilion as a classic case of 'consensus compromise', though a considerable improvement on British efforts at past Expos. Banham's attempt (in his *New Society* article of 1974) to identify the characteristics that underlay Powell & Moya's success makes fascinating reading. 'They have an uncanny and seemingly uncontrived ability to sense the mood of place and time – and client ... The P&M constituency relishes niceties of professional skill, rather than grand gestures'. Powell & Moya's buildings were not just designed in tune with their sites: 'they have a knack of looking as if they were the buildings that actually established the character, rather than the ones that simply followed it'. For Banham, it was the apparent effortlessness of Powell & Moya's work that impressed, and that made them the true creators of a convincingly British modern architecture: 'more famous architects tried very hard to fulfil this programme – Gibberd at London Airport, Spence at Coventry Cathedral – and have screwed it up because they tried *too* hard. By "not going out of their way", Powell & Moya have achieved it again and again.' Powell & Moya's work was, said Banham, 'gentlemanly' – and very British[16] – and none the worse for it.

Powell & Moya was well on the way to becoming a British institution. But the seventies would be a decade in which the architectural consensus established in the immediate post-war years crumbled. Postmodernism, community architecture and Neoclassicism were part of a bewilderingly diverse scene. Nonetheless, the key works of the decade were to be Rogers & Piano's Pompidou Centre and Norman Foster's Willis Faber offices at Ipswich. By the end of the decade, Rogers and Foster were building Lloyd's of London and the Hong Kong and Shanghai Bank. Even architectural practices with the status of national institutions could not rest on their laurels.

Notes

1   Philip Powell, 'No visible means of support: Skylon and the South Bank', *Twentieth Century Architecture,* 5, 2001, p84.
2   Hidalgo Moya, 'The Skylon': typescript in Powell & Moya archive.
3   ibid.
4   Philip Powell, op. cit., pp84–5.
5   *New Statesman,* 5 May 1951.
6   *The Times,* 18 April 1951.
7   Simon Houfe, *Sir Albert Richardson – the Professor* (Luton, 1980), p186.
8   Philip Powell, op. cit., p86.
9   'Chichester Festival Theatre', *Architects' Journal,* 4 July 1962, p36.
10   Michael Webb, *Architecture in Britain Today* (London, 1969), p199.
11   'Britain at Expo', *Architects' Journal,* 22 April 1970, p970.
12   Robin Boyd, 'Expo and exhibitionism', *Architectural Review,* August 1970, p99.
13   *Building,* 24 April 1970, p84.
14   *Architects' Journal,* 22 April 1970, p979.
15   ibid., p977.
16   Reyner Banham, 'Nice, modern and British!', *New Society,* 18 July 1974, pp160–1.

CHAPTER THREE:
Oxbridge and Beyond

Housing, health and education were the foundations on which the Labour government elected in 1945 (to the delight of Philip Powell and Jacko Moya) began to build the Welfare State. Powell & Moya had been launched, spectacularly, on the basis of Britain's largest public-housing project. Although housing did not become, after the completion of Churchill Gardens, a mainstay of the practice, both education and health (the latter in particular, right through to the 1990s) figured hugely in its workload. Indeed, the firm was able to exist for half a century with scarcely any work outside the public sector – a fact that the founding partners, at least, never regretted.

The post-war school-building programme had its roots in the tempestuous world of architectural education in the 1930s (when the AA was rent between traditionalists and socially minded Modernists – the latter eventually winning the day, and creating the ethos in which Philip Powell and Jacko Moya came to maturity). The Butler Education Act of 1944, enacted before the Labour election victory, provided another stimulus to school building, with its guarantee of secondary education for all. Led by Hertfordshire, with its heroic development programme launched by Stirrat Johnson-Marshall (later chief architect at the Ministry of Education), local authorities responded to the urgent need for new schools. Michael Powell left Powell & Moya in 1950 to join the housing division in the LCC Architect's Department, then led by Robert Matthew, and became its Schools Architect in 1956. The school-building programme was, above all, a triumph for public-sector architects, but there was work too for private practices – Yorke Rosenberg and Mardall (YRM); Architects' Co-Partnership; Ernö Goldfinger; H. T. Cadbury-Brown; Denys Lasdun; and Chamberlin, Powell and Bon were all commissioned to design schools in London during the 1950s. Powell & Moya's Mayfield School, completed in 1955 for the LCC with Bob Henley as architect in charge, was one of the most notable of these projects.

Ian Nairn described Mayfield as 'one of the best modern buildings in Britain', praising its 'burning humanity, its devotion to the job it has to do and the avoidance of any kind of self-conscious architectural effect. There is plenty of architectural effect, but it is natural and integral.'[1] Powell & Moya's task was to expand an existing girls' grammar school, founded in 1907 and catering for 500 pupils, to a comprehensive

Opposite: The Cripps Building of St John's College, Cambridge

The disciplined and elegant exterior of one of the teaching blocks at Mayfield School, Putney, completed in 1955

with 2,100 girls, retaining the existing Edwardian buildings and working them into a rational plan for the 3.5-hectare (9-acre) site at West Hill, Putney. Schools on this scale were virtually unknown in Britain – in fact, only the larger public schools, such as Eton College, could boast such numbers. Moreover, the very concept of comprehensive secondary education was both novel and highly controversial. The post-war Labour government remained faithful to a tripartite system of grammar, secondary modern and technical schools – catering, it was argued, for the needs both of the academic and the more practically minded – and it was left to individual local authorities, such as the LCC, to advance the comprehensive cause. There was no clear direction as to how these large new institutions should be treated architecturally – in 1956, *Architectural Design* reported that 'it was inevitable that the first comprehensive schools should show some hesitation and irresolution in their architectural character'.[2] One approach was to build high. Nairn enthused about Tulse Hill School, designed by the LCC Architects, with all its classrooms housed in an 'awe-inspiring' nine-storey slab (the school has now been demolished), but this model was not widely emulated.

One aspect of the Mayfield project that generated intense interest – and was extensively documented in the professional press from its inception – was its modest cost: under £350,000. An allowable cost of £250 per place had been budgeted for the school, but it was completed at a price of £178 per place. The site for the expanded school embraced land freed up by wartime bombing, and there were a number of mature trees which were, as far as possible, retained. In contrast to the irregular layout of the existing school buildings, Powell & Moya's additions were arranged on strictly orthogonal lines at the heart of the site – with three classroom blocks of three storeys each extending off a central assembly hall, and a separate gymnasium block to the west. In contrast to the Tulse Hill approach, Mayfield reflected a strategy of humanising the comprehensive by breaking it down into manageable units.

The *Architectural Association Journal* felt that the external effect of the new buildings was more successful than its 'hard, mechanistic' interiors.[3] In fact, the low cost of the project, and the fact that it was completed ahead of schedule, was the result of a hard-headed approach to construction, using relatively traditional techniques and eschewing the use of a standardised system. The teaching blocks used load-bearing brick cross- and end-walls, rather than a framed structure – this at the time of a continuing steel shortage – with floors of pre-stressed concrete planks. Internally, they were all arranged with rooms along central corridors (not overlong but necessarily devoid of natural light): a practical and economical diagram. Externally, the blocks were clad in a bespoke system with timber frames housing metal-framed window units – a pragmatic approach typical of Powell & Moya which, thanks to careful detailing,

Interior of the assembly hall block at
Mayfield School, Putney

Metal-framed windows at Mayfield School, set in timber frames

produced an extremely elegant aesthetic. The central assembly hall block, also used for dining, was, according to the *AA Journal*, 'fine, majestic and exciting'.[4] Sliding screens allowed the principal space to be expanded to seat 1,800 – a device that subsequently proved difficult to utilise. This block was steel-framed, its roof structure consisting of two space frames covered in hardwood boarding, their ends resting on rolled steel columns that were left uncased and painted. The steel shortage appears to have kicked in again by the time the gymnasium block, housing three spaces with changing rooms in between them, was designed, since great exposed timber trusses of African mahogany spanning 11 metres (36 feet) were used here for the roof structure. Revisiting the school five years after its opening, the *AJ* found its principal defect to be that of communications – the decentralised plan meant regular, time-wasting movements of pupils and staff across the site. There was also a worrying problem with the deflection of the roof trusses in the gymnasium block, while the studded rubber floors used extensively in the buildings had largely worn out and were being replaced with linoleum. Generally, however, the school was 'standing up well to hard and efficient use'.[5] Today, its merits can only be appreciated via photographs, since Powell & Moya's buildings were radically and disastrously altered in the 1980s by Wandsworth Council.

A much later, and less well-known, school project by Powell & Moya, Plumstead

Eton College dining hall exterior

Manor Comprehensive, completed in 1973 for the GLC, involved a similar mix of existing and new buildings. Indeed, in this project, designed at a time when old buildings were increasingly valued, the restored King's Warren School of 1913 was given a pivotal role in the development of the site. New, low-rise buildings were laid out in small blocks linked by corridors around landscaped courtyards. As Sherban Cantacuzino commented in the *AR*, these blocks 'are not just domestic in scale; they could, quite simply, *be* housing'. The extensive use of brick and pitched roofs reflected Powell & Moya's 'deep concern with the place they build in'.[6] Contemporary with the Plumstead project came a commission (in 1973) from a very different school: Eton College. The brief was to provide a refectory for boys and a university-style common room, with bar and restaurant, for masters. The site was a garden close to the heart of Eton. The building – initially known prosaically as 'the central feeding building', later 'Bekynton' – is an elegant single-storey, steel-framed structure with covered walkways extending around enclosed courts, the interiors illuminated by monopitch clerestories. 'Admirably crisp' is the *Buildings of England*'s comment.[7]

While Mayfield School neared completion, Powell & Moya became involved with the first of a series of projects for Oxford and Cambridge colleges. Brasenose College, founded in 1509, was neither the largest nor the most prestigious of Oxford's colleges

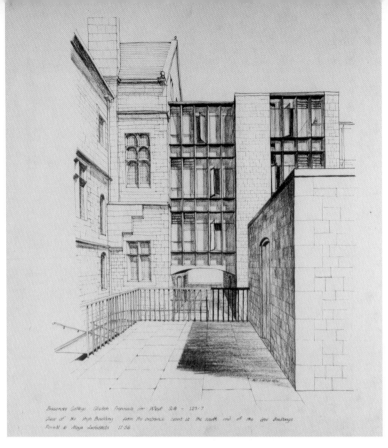

Brasenose College sketch
proposal, dating from 1956

Interior of a student room,
as designed in the first
scheme for Brasenose
College

– it had long been renowned for sporting, rather than academic, prowess. However, it occupied a site close to the very heart of the city, wedged between the High Street and the Bodleian Library and with Gibbs's Radcliffe Camera and the University church of St Mary as near neighbours. Towards the end of the 19th century, the architect Sir Thomas ('Graham') Jackson had extended the college towards the High Street, where his elaborately decorated Gothic frontage is often assumed by the uninitiated to be genuinely medieval. Wedged into the west by Lincoln College, Brasenose ('BNC', as it is always known in Oxford) had little space for further growth, but there was a small L-shaped sliver of land behind the shops on the High Street and to the west of Jackson's splendid New Quadrangle, which had acquired the nickname of 'the Arab Quarter'. The Baroque church of All Saints, later converted into a library for Lincoln College, loomed over the wall. Philip Powell recalled a gloomy area 'filled with decomposing lavatories and baths', a truly dilapidated backyard. The genesis of the building project that was to occupy this unpromising space came as early as 1954. Derek Stow, who worked on the project in its early stages with Philip Powell, recalls that the college wanted a building that would last 200 years. The client brief, wrote Powell, was simply to 'fit in, squeeze in, as many rooms as you can without being anti-social about it'.[8]

The mid fifties was a period of transition for architecture in Oxford. In the immediate post-war years, the University was still completing laboratory buildings in a broadly traditional style by Hubert Worthington, Lanchester & Lodge and others. Sir Edward Maufe's Dolphin Quad at St John's College was a competent, if lifeless, exercise in pre-war Neoclassicism. The new buildings of Nuffield College, a bizarrely stretched reprise of Cotswold vernacular completed in 1962 to designs by Austen Harrison, were described by the authors of *New Oxford*, a guide to new buildings in the city prepared by a group of students, as 'Oxford's biggest monument to barren reaction'. J. M. Richards in the *AR* called Nuffield 'a missed opportunity of a really tragic kind'.[9] In this climate, the completion of the 'Beehive' building at St John's in 1960, with a further scheme by Maufe (who was an honorary fellow of the college) dropped in favour of designs by Architects' Co-Partnership, seemed a major breakthrough and paved the way for the rout of the traditionalists. The prime mover in the Beehive project was a young don, Howard Colvin, subsequently to become the best-known architectural historian of his day but no advocate of historicism in new architecture.

The building boom that gripped Oxford from the late fifties on was largely driven by the demand for more residential accommodation for students. Not only were numbers growing (up to 9,500 by 1965) but there was also a consensus that undergraduates should be able to spend at least two years of their time at Oxford living in college – before the Second World War, over half of the undergraduate population was obliged to live in extramural lodgings. It was clear that the new accommodation could not duplicate that in existing buildings dating from the 14th to the 19th centuries: 'sets' were out, bedsits in.

It remains unclear why Brasenose chose Powell & Moya, and college archives give no evidence that anything approaching a selection process was established, though

The Arab Quarter at Brasenose College, the site for Powell & Moya's new buildings, was a dismal backyard

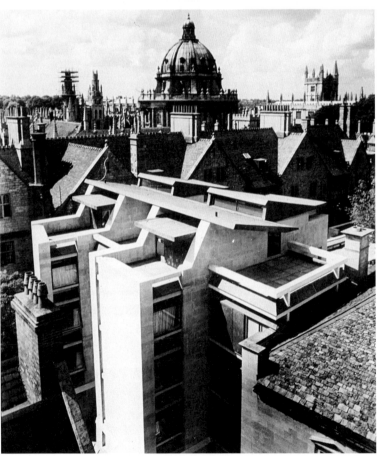

Powell & Moya's new residential buildings at Brasenose College, Oxford were intended as 'another piece of the existing jumble'

the installation around this time of a new bursar, Norman Leyland – his predecessor had been in office since 1929 – was probably significant. Leyland had been appointed Fellow in Economics in 1947. He had an astute grasp of finance, enjoyed playing the stock market and proved an excellent manager of the college's finances – BNC was not a rich college. He was also modern-minded, a lover of jazz and of modern architecture – a member, it seems, of an exclusive club of like-minded dons that included David Henderson of Lincoln College (later a professor at University College London). Leyland went on to become first director of the Oxford Centre for Management Studies (founded in 1965). He approached Powell & Moya to design the Centre's building, which became Templeton College, but Philip Powell declined the job on the grounds that the practice had too much work, and recommended his former assistant, Richard Burton, as architect – Leyland subsequently moved into a house designed by Burton's practice.

The formal decision to commission development proposals for the Arab Quarter site at BNC was taken by the college's governing body in December 1955. By the following February, Powell & Moya was the chosen practice. Early sketches for the new building show something distinctly removed from what was eventually built. It was to be clad in traditional Oxford stone, perhaps the Clipsham limestone popularised by T. G. Jackson towards the end of the 19th century. Although unequivocally modern, the building was to feature a type of mullioned window. The overall form of the building was to be rigidly rectilinear. In 1957, Richard Burton joined Powell & Moya, and after working (with Paul Koralek for a time) on the nurses' housing at the new Swindon hospital was in due course put in charge of the Oxford project under Jacko Moya, following on from Robert Huddleston. Burton, later a founding partner in the practice of Ahrends

Plan of the ground floor of the additions to Brasenose College

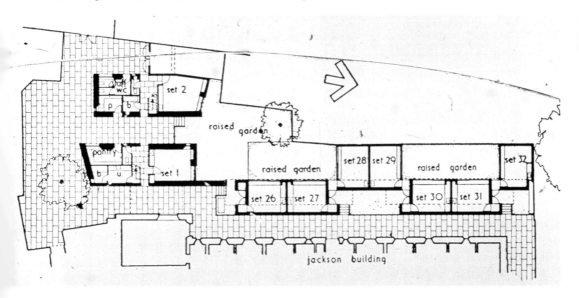

Burton Koralek, had come from the LCC after training at the AA. His contribution to the evolution of the project was undoubtedly considerable. (The third partner in ABK, German-born, South African-raised Peter Ahrends, though never formally employed by Powell & Moya, designed much of the furniture for Brasenose.) Burton recalls reworking the scheme – 'the first version was a mess' – with Moya, though Powell was also much involved. Planning consent was given in 1959, after an unexpected referral to the Royal Fine Art Commission, and the scheme went on site with locally based N. Collisson Ltd as contractors. The nature of the site produced strained relations with neighbours. Lincoln College complained about noise from the construction works and the collapse of a wall, which destroyed a compost heap belonging to its Rector.

The new buildings at Brasenose College were clad in Portland stone, rather than the Oxford stone originally envisaged

Blue Boar Quad at Christ Church, Oxford, soon after completion

In fact, though the site was very confined, it presented a challenge that the architects rather relished. 'We tried to treat the new work not as a separate building but as another piece of the existing jumble,' Philip Powell commented later.[10] It was imperative to capitalise on such views as were available and to maximise natural light within the 32 student rooms provided. An irregular plan was the result, with most of the rooms accommodated in a four-storey block consisting of two 'bastions' (each with its own staircase and connected only at ground- and top-floor level) at the south end of the site, close to the High Street and overlooking the churchyard of All Saints. The narrower strip extending along the rear of the New Quad contains a series of one-storey pavilions, with rooms approached through small entrance courts. Like the Beehives at St John's, the buildings are faced in Portland, rather than Oxford, stone – in fact, the stone walls are load-bearing, not a veneer – with sliding plate-glass windows and plentiful use of lead sheet on external surfaces. Inside, one shower or bath was provided for every eight students – 'quite enough', it was argued by the college.

The strongly modelled form of the buildings reflected a break with Powell & Moya's previous work, and with initial ideas for Brasenose – indeed, not everyone warmed to the 'peculiar' geometry of the building, though *New Oxford* judged it 'one of the most important post-war contributions to Oxford's architectural heritage'.[11] There are clear hints in the scheme of the direction in which ABK was to move – Richard Burton left Powell & Moya when the new practice was launched in 1961. Peter Skinner recalls the project as one that, whatever its satisfactions, 'made us no money'. However, it soon acquired a reputation as a highly innovative intervention into a historic context, and the

CHRIST CHURCH   OXFORD   NEW BUILDINGS   INTERIOR of A TYPICAL BED-SITTING ROOM Powell & Moya 155/24

Perspective by Moya of the interior of a typical bed-sitting room in Blue Boar Quad at Christ Church

college was swamped by visiting parties of architects, students and planners. George Pace, the York architect then working on designs for a new library at Durham University, came at the suggestion of the Dean of Durham (a BNC man) – it is not hard to detect the influence of Powell & Moya in the building he completed there in 1966. So did the Master of St John's College, Cambridge, which had already appointed Powell & Moya as the architects for a much larger new building, funded by an alumnus of the college.

Brasenose proved to be a problematic project for Powell & Moya: here, as elsewhere, innovative design was out of step with the building technology of the day. By 1965, there were complaints that lead sheeting was detaching itself from the walls and damp was soon penetrating through roofs. Moya came to the college to discuss the problems, bringing with him Powell & Moya's regular engineering consultant, Charles Weiss – 'a very tough customer', the bursar commented. In due course, the problems were resolved, though not before the architects had made an *ex gratia* payment of £1,000 towards the cost of repairs.

Picture of a student room in
Blue Boar Quad at Christ Church

A Staircase in Blue Boar Quad

The commission from Christ Church, Oxford, to design a more substantial residential development came directly out of the Brasenose job. The college, one of the largest and wealthiest in Oxford, wanted accommodation for around 60 undergraduates in study bedrooms, with eight sets for eight research fellows. The site, mostly used for parking, was long and narrow, extending 90 metres (300 feet) along Blue Boar Street, a narrow thoroughfare, perhaps best known for the Bear pub, separating the northern edge of Christ Church from the Town Hall. On the edge of it was the Old Brewhouse, a listed building that had to be retained. Other structures there were cleared.

Discussions with Oxford planners produced an immediate difference of opinion. The planners wanted the stone wall along Blue Boar Street demolished, so that the street could be widened. Powell & Moya resisted: 'Instead, the wall remained imperforate,' wrote Philip Powell, 'and was used as a podium for a low superstructure of north-facing staircases, landings and bathrooms following its curve but broken up into small "towers", a kind of castellated coping. Here is a setting of street, not college architecture, yet with a hint of collegiate life behind – a common event in Oxford.'[12] The *AR* liked the way in which the new development, completed in 1968, broke with the monumentality of Christ Church, being arranged as an irregular quad of almost medieval character, 'separate, distinct, organic'. It used much the same palette of materials as the Brasenose scheme – Portland stone for load-bearing walls and dominant vertical buttresses, lead

The Picture Gallery at Christ Church was designed to slot into the Dean's Garden with minimum disruption

panels and exposed concrete floor slabs – but the aesthetic was stretched sideways, producing, it was felt, 'a looser and for that reason lesser architecture'.[13] Student rooms were placed on three floors, with rooftop sets for research fellows arranged as pavilions in order to produce, along with the strongly modelled water tank housings, a castellated roofline of decidedly picturesque aspect (which Pevsner, who admired the scheme, felt was a trifle self-indulgent). The interior of the site was excavated by around 1.2 metres (4 feet) in order to allow for the requisite height, while restricting the impact of the building on Blue Boar Street. Rooms were grouped around four stairs, with each landing serving three rooms, and with bathrooms, WCs and pantries at half-landing level. As at Brasenose, the Christ Church development was to suffer from practical problems, especially with regard to roof coverings, which led the college to consider possible demolition. That option closed when Blue Boar Quad was listed at Grade II*. In 2008, a major refurbishment scheme by Purcell Miller Tritton, including upgrading of all rooms with en-suite bathrooms, was under way and promised to give the buildings a century or two of useful life.

Blue Boar Quad shared much of the language of Powell & Moya's largest Oxbridge project, the Cripps Building at St John's, Cambridge – the timescale of the two schemes overlapped in the office. From Christ Church, however, there was another commission, producing one of the practice's most satisfying buildings. Christ Church's outstanding

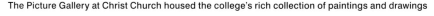

The Picture Gallery at Christ Church housed the college's rich collection of paintings and drawings

art collection, included not only a splendid array of paintings, chiefly by Italian 'primitives', but also around 2,000 drawings which were the real glory of the collection. The aim was to provide a place where this collection could be safely conserved and also shown to the public. The only site available was the Dean's Garden, which lay to the east of the great Tom Quad. One assumes that the then Dean was happy with the invasion of his private domain, for Powell & Moya's project preserved much of the amenity of the garden, sinking the new gallery into the verdant lawns. Philip Powell, who was particularly fond of this project, wrote:

> a tunnel burrows its way through the basement, suddenly revealing a glassed-in cloister around a lawn and the interior of the main Gallery itself, half-sunk into the Dean's garden, white, top-lit and of stone, plaster, concrete and wood. Outside and unseen by the public the lowered Gallery is a rough stone wall no higher than the garden walls which surround it. A

Entrance to the Picture Gallery at Christ Church

The additions to Corpus Christi College, Oxford, were more modest than Powell & Moya's projects at Brasenose College and Christ Church

series of sunken, ramped and elevated lawns, weaving their way around and over the Gallery, give the Dean his garden back.[14]

Inside, the aesthetic is one of bare plaster, stone and tiled floors: rather too monastic, one reviewer felt, especially for Tintoretto and Van Dyck. There was too little space, some felt, for displaying drawings (in a tiny, artificially lit strongroom). Nonetheless, 40 years on, in the aftermath of many art museum projects in which the works of art seem a lesser consideration than the ego of the architect, the Christ Church Picture Gallery has aged gracefully. Indeed, it prefigured a series of gallery projects, including those by Louis Kahn and Renzo Piano, in which architecture and art coexist without deference on either side.

Compared to the work at Brasenose and Christ Church, Powell & Moya's addition to Corpus Christi College, completed in 1969, is a more modest proposition. With 41

The new addition at Corpus Christi College attempts to blend with the established street scene

The foyer to the dining hall and common room block at Wolfson College is clad in white marble, the gift of Sir Isaac Wolfson

study bedrooms, the building overlooks Magpie Lane but is accessed from the rear. It is seen to best advantage at roof level, where a varied roofscape provides interest. At street level, it is still possible to regret the loss of the early 19th-century houses demolished to make way for the development.

It may seem surprising that Powell & Moya was not commissioned for one of the new universities which so transformed British higher education in the 1960s. The explanation might be found in the sheer volume of work that the practice was handling at the time, notably at Oxford and Cambridge and in the hospital field – 'it restricted the amount of new work we could decently take on', Philip Powell recalled. Some idea of how the firm might have tackled such a commission can be gained from Wolfson College, which occupies a self-contained campus in north Oxford. The foundation of the college as a graduate society, camping out in a series of old houses, reflected the rapid increase during the post-war years in the number of postgraduate students at Oxford, especially in science subjects. The aim of Wolfson's founding members was to establish a permanent graduate college, where there could also be accommodation for married graduates and their families. Initially known as Iffley College, it was to occupy a picturesque site in the village of the same name – unfortunately far too remote from the centre of Oxford to be a practical base. After Professor (later Sir) Isaiah Berlin was

Wolfson College occupies a former garden site in North Oxford, close to the river Cherwell

elected (in 1966) as the college's first president, £1.5 million of funding was secured from the Wolfson Foundation for the buildings, to be erected on a site donated by the University off Banbury Road and close to the River Cherwell. Berlin sensibly sought advice on the appointment of architects. Nikolaus Pevsner suggested Powell & Moya as one suitable 'outstanding' practice. A selection committee was subsequently formed and visits made to new university buildings in Britain and abroad. In Finland, they met Alvar Aalto (disliking his use of 'harsh red brick'). The search extended to the USA, where visits were made to Princeton, Yale and other campuses: 'The journeys in Britain alone extended to almost 4,000 miles.'[15] The resulting shortlist was somewhat eccentric, consisting of Gordon Bunshaft of Skidmore, Owings and Merrill (architect of the Beinecke Library at Yale), the Finnish husband-and-wife team of Heikki and Kaija Siren (best known for their work at the University of Technology in Otaniemi), and the practice of Powell & Moya. The appointment of Powell & Moya (in May 1967) came after the firm had been selected as architects for the prestigious British Pavilion at the Osaka Expo, due to be held in 1970.

By January 1968, the large Victorian house at the centre of the site had been demolished, and in May the Queen laid the foundation stone. The buildings were completed

The interior of the library at Wolfson College, Oxford

The landscape scheme at Wolfson College included a punt dock

Interior of the timber-lined dining hall at Wolfson College, Oxford

The unbuilt project for Oxford's Pitt Rivers Museum, designed in collaboration with Pier Luigi Nervi, would have replaced a group of Victorian buildings

in 1974. Sir Isaac Wolfson, the benefactor whose foundation had made them possible, took a close interest in the project. Interviewed in 1993, Philip Powell recalled Wolfson's desire for 'some show of lavishness', which he was prepared to fund from his own pocket. There was the idea, for example, of red marble cladding for the entrance hall, which Powell thought would make it look 'like a posh bank'. Wolfson's generous instincts were redirected instead towards funding the fine white marble, chaste but costly, which forms the floors, balustrades and stairs in the foyer to the dining hall and common rooms.

It was Berlin who influenced the basic plan of the college. Powell & Moya's proposed plan reflected their by now famous capacity for responding to context, capitalising on the potential of the site and retaining existing landscape, including mature trees. A punt harbour extending off the river was one of the more enjoyable elements of the revamped landscape, bringing the water closer to the buildings. To the south, the harbour was enclosed by 'B' block, a four-storey building cranked in plan. Berlin disliked the cranked form and suggested the building should be curved instead. The architects were initially resistant, but Berlin persisted. From his holiday home in the Ligurian resort of Portofino, he 'bombarded' them with postcards showing the harbour there, with its run of curved buildings along the water. 'Let me persuade you to some gentle inclination to a shape less stiff,' he wrote. 'Rectilinear rigours', he insisted, were out of tune with the site.[16] Eventually the architects gave in and the block was redesigned, though Moya was unhappy with the results. Internally, the most significant spaces were the long, thin, top-lit library and the timber-lined dining hall, the precursor of that at Queens' College, Cambridge, which omitted the usual high table in a reflection of the egalitarian aspirations of the college.

Geoffrey Tyack, comparing the romantic planning of Wolfson with the rigid ratio-
nalism of Arne Jacobsen's St Catherine's and praising the integration of Powell & Moya's
buildings with the landscape, nonetheless found the architecture of Wolfson 'somewhat
monotonous'.[17] Yet the college remains, later additions notwithstanding, one of the major
works of the practice and an expression of its commitment to humanity and appropriateness over mere display.

One major Oxford project remained unbuilt. In 1967, Powell & Moya was commissioned to work with the great Italian engineer Pier Luigi Nervi on a new building for the
Pitt Rivers Museum, an extraordinary anthropological and archaeological collection
given to Oxford University in 1884 and housed in an adjunct to the Victorian Gothic
University Museum. The designs, for a circular building with a tropical garden housed
beneath a glazed dome at its centre, reflected the curatorial programme – to present
material in a typological sequence, as the museum's founder, Lt-General Pitt Rivers,
had always intended. The project was not uncontroversial, since it involved demolishing
existing Victorian buildings on Banbury Road, but its abandonment – the requisite
funding was not forthcoming – was lamented by Howard Colvin, who wrote: 'the
project was, perhaps, the last chance for the University to build in the twentieth century
something that would take its place with the Divinity School, the Radcliffe Library and
the Ashmolean Museum as a major work of European architecture'.[18]

A typically bold perspective by Jacko Moya of the first proposal for the Cripps Building at
St John's College, Cambridge

Looking East from main entrance inside the new buildings   Powell+Moya

The Cripps Building occupies a green site on the fringe of the college

England's other ancient university seemed, for a time, to have taken the lead over Oxford as a patron of new architecture. 'Cambridge', wrote Pevsner, 'is one of the happiest hunting-grounds in Britain for specimens of the architectural style and fashions of the nineteen-sixties.'[19] Like Oxford, the University had grown (to over 10,000 students by 1967) and there was a demand for more residential accommodation. In 1956, Leslie Martin, Chief Architect to the London County Council, had become head of the University's department of architecture (Oxford famously declined to teach architecture). He was to exercise a potent influence on new university architecture across the country (recommending Chamberlin, Powell and Bon, for instance, to masterplan the expansion of Leeds University). When St John's College was offered a remarkably generous benefaction by an old 'Johnian', Humphrey Cripps (1915–2000), Martin was one authority consulted. Cripps's family business was in the manufacture of pianos but he had amassed a fortune by diversifying into motor parts, employing over 1,000 people in his Northampton works. Cripps had developed an association with Nottingham University, where he entirely funded the construction of Cripps Hall, a hall of residence on the campus designed by the Neoclassicist practice of McMorran and Whitby and completed in 1959 at a cost of over £400,000. St John's had launched a development appeal, both to refurbish and modernise its existing residences and to build new ones. In 1958 Cripps offered 'to deal with the new buildings part of the appeal'. The then master, Sir James Wordie (who had been Cripps's tutor at the college), wrote of the offer: 'we must show immediate appreciation: this may be the largest benefaction the college has ever received'.[20] Cripps's approach was initially cautious. By the end of 1959, he had offered £75,000 with an equal sum in a year's time – his donation was eventually to top £1 million. Donald McMorran, he suggested, might be a suitable architect for the new buildings. A deputation from St John's, led by the new master, the Rev. J. S. Boys-Smith, went to see Cripps Hall – its reactions are not recorded, but Leslie Martin was already being consulted both on the siting of the building and on the selection of an architect. This would clearly not be a tradition-alist if Martin had his way. The site was a fairly obvious choice: a parcel of land owned by the college at Fishponds Close, north of the 1830s Gothic Revival New Court and Magdalene College's Benson Court designed by Sir Edwin Lutyens close to the end of the Backs where the Bin Brook flows into the River Cam. Martin advised against an

The roof terraces at the Cripps Building provided an enjoyable spot for socialising

open competition, but suggested that a shortlist of practices be invited to present ideas. Members of the college's governing body were asked for suggestions. Interestingly, one of the first names put forward was that of the young Cedric Price, who had graduated from the college as recently as 1955 and had as yet built nothing. David Roberts and Hughes & Bicknell, both with a strong track record in Cambridge, were more practical suggestions. The names of Arne Jacobsen, Sir Hugh Casson (another Johnian), RMJM and Leslie Martin himself also featured on the list. Early the following year, Sir Nikolaus Pevsner (who had held a fellowship at St John's while Slade Professor of Fine Art at Cambridge between 1949 and 1955) submitted a list of possible architects, including Powell & Moya, Denys Lasdun, Chamberlin, Powell and Bon, Architects' Co-Partnership, Denis Clarke Hall and James Cubitt. Martin added the names of James Stirling and Alison and Peter Smithson, the leading advocates of the 'New Brutalism'. As the deliberations progressed, those of a number of eminent foreign architects featured: from the USA, Louis Kahn, Gordon Bunshaft of SOM and Philip Johnson;

A covered route, with access to staircases, forms the ground floor of the Cripps Building at St John's College

Humphrey Cripps, funder of the Cripps Building at St John's, went on to fund a major addition to
Queens' College, Cambridge

Italy's BBPR and Ignazio Gardella; and Alvar Aalto from Finland. Aalto was a significant
influence already on Leslie Martin and his assistant Colin St John Wilson, and since
Martin was due to visit Finland in the summer of 1961 he undertook to approach the
eminent Finn. Pevsner was doubtful: Aalto, he told the master, was 'not an easy man to
pin down'. In due course, Martin reported that Aalto 'would not commit himself' and
regrettably would have to be discounted.[21]

The selection process for St John's Cripps Building is remarkably well-documented
and reflects the ambition of the college to acquire a building of outstanding quality.
Chamberlin, Powell and Bon, masterplanners of the Leeds campus, and Richard
Sheppard, appointed architect of the new Churchill College in July 1959, were judged to
be too busy. Max Fry's practice was 'not as good as it used to be'. Andrew Renton, who
had worked with Basil Spence on the Erasmus Building at Queens' College, was simply
'not the man'. By August 1961, Aalto having been finally ruled out, it was resolved to
approach Lasdun and Powell & Moya, and both made their initial presentations in

October. The final presentations took place on 24 April 1962. The governing body met on 4 May and a vote was taken: for Lasdun, 22; for Powell & Moya, 28. A week later, a better-attended meeting produced 29 votes for Lasdun and 35 for Powell & Moya, who were subsequently invited to undertake the project. Lasdun's proposal, with echoes of the 'ziggurats' he was to build for the University of East Anglia, consisted of four pyramidal blocks linked by walkways, and would have been at odds with the context of the Backs. (Indeed, Lasdun does not appear at his best in Cambridge – his projects for Christ's and Fitzwilliam colleges, both only partly realised, are among his weakest works.)

The Cripps Building was a major extension to St John's, the largest since the completion of New Court, with accommodation for 200 undergraduates (a mix of study bedrooms and two-room sets), plus eight larger sets for Fellows. Typically for Oxbridge, space standards were considerably higher than those in other universities – the then University Grants Committee norm was 11 square metres (120 square feet) for a study bedroom, while those in the Cripps Building were half as big again. Rooms were arranged in the traditional way, on staircases with bathrooms and WCs on the same floor. The building was designed for a long life – Mr Cripps specified 500 years and was prepared to pay for high-quality materials – but the college wanted an element of flexibility (which was lacking in the Brasenose project). Hence, structural cross-walls were dispensed with in favour of a concrete frame with columns (housing ducts) along the perimeter of the building supporting in-situ floor slabs. Internal partitions were of non-structural blockwork. Externally, the building was faced in Powell & Moya's (by now) favoured mix of Roach and Whitbed Portland stone. As at Brasenose, what attracted critical attention was the architects' response to place and their ability to work in context in a frankly modern manner. The building was arranged as a sinuous line, snaking across the site from the Cam on the east, where it reached down to a punt dock on the river, towards the ancient School of Pythagoras (long pre-dating the college) on the west. While not arranged in the form of traditional courtyards, the building evoked the atmosphere of the classic Cambridge court. As Philip Powell explained, 'whilst never containing courtyards itself, it gives the effect of courtyards by its confronta-tions with other buildings or with other parts of itself, continuing the collegiate pattern of court following court established by older parts of the college'.[22] A covered route extended along the building at ground-floor level. Projecting bay windows allowed the rooms to take full advantage of the varying views.

The Cripps Building remains a magnificent climax to the superb sequence of spaces that form St John's. A photograph taken at the opening party in 1967, with mini-skirted girls sipping champagne on the roof of the building (now closed off on health-and-safety grounds), captures its optimism and sheer style. The critics were unstinting in their praise. Pevsner described Cripps as 'a masterpiece by one of the best architectural partnerships in the country'.[23] For the young bloods at *Cambridge New Architecture* (the third edition appeared in 1970) the building, however, was in some respects problematic. It was simply too traditional: 'by its very nature it reinforces the glorious

The dining hall at Queens' College, Cambridge, when new. Part of the additions to the college funded by Humphrey Cripps

The addition of a top floor to Powell & Moya's Cripps Court at Queens' College was driven by the need for space but compromises the purity of the architecture

tradition of Cambridge, and in so doing it has fossilized a situation irrevocably that in the not so distant future may seem intolerable ... the attitude which created this building may ultimately accelerate Cambridge's decline'.[24]

This prediction, one might suggest, proved mistaken: neither St John's nor Cambridge has declined in the last 40 years – indeed, both have thrived. Not that Cripps was problem-free. Its underfloor heating proved too expensive to operate and was replaced by conventional radiators. The concealed service ducts have produced serious maintenance problems. There was the usual issue of flat-roof failure, addressed during the 1980s but about to be tackled again, at the time of writing, by a comprehensive and costly refurbishment project that will also provide en-suite bathrooms throughout – as much for the benefit of the lucrative conference trade as the students. In 1987, after long deliberation, the one-storey block containing a Junior Combination Room which formed a link to Cripps on the route from New Court was demolished and replaced by the ungainly Fisher Building, designed by Saunders Boston, an exercise in pitch-roofed Postmodernism.

The success of the St John's project led Humphrey Cripps to commission Powell & Moya in 1971 for a second Cambridge scheme, at Queens' College. The architects came with the offer of the funding, and the college was given no choice in the matter and was not even aware of the budget, since Cripps managed the project, directing the contractors personally. 'He took a great interest in the project, even visiting our site Portacabins to review aspects of the ongoing design and telling risqué jokes,' recalls Roger Burr, who joined Powell & Moya in 1969 as a newly qualified architect (he had had a summer job in the office while still at school) and later became a partner, working on the second phase of the Queens' project. Burr recalls Jacko Moya as a very much hands-on partner in charge, attending weekly meetings – and enjoying spare moments punting on the Cam. The site was the last one available anywhere on the Backs, across the river from the picturesque older buildings of the college and behind Queens' College's Fisher Building (Neo-Tudor of the 1930s and memorably described by Pevsner as 'looking exactly like a friendly block of flats at, say, Pinner').[25] Again, the project was a large one: 146 student rooms, some fellows' sets and a new dining hall to seat 250. The scheme was completed in three phases: the first in 1975; the second phase, including the dining hall, in 1978. (The final phase, including sports facilities, was completed only in 1989, to designs by locally based Bland, Brown & Cole.) In contrast to the romantic and irregular layout of the St John's building, that at Queens', laid out around a square court, is highly formal and rigidly orthogonal, deliberately continuing the sequence of existing courts. As at St John's, structural cross-walls were replaced by a framed structure, allowing for long-term flexibility. The structure was expressed at Queens' as a framework of exposed, hammered concrete columns, which used a white aggregate, supporting floor slabs and sills – producing an aesthetic that some have judged too severe for the context of the Backs. The contrast between Cripps Court and the warm red brick of the older buildings at Queens' is certainly dramatic. The critic Stephen Gardiner, who was always generous to Powell & Moya, felt that their work at Queens' was 'easily the best piece of modern architecture by a British architect anywhere', yet there is a precise, even slightly clinical quality to Cripps Court that is not present in any of the other Oxbridge projects.[26]

The finest element in the scheme is undoubtedly the dining hall, with its dramatic roof structure, delicately engineered and clad in warmly textured timber – impressive, but at the same time intimate and a really successful reinterpretation of the traditional Cambridge hall. Powell & Moya was always good at designing social spaces and the geniality of the practice shone through at Queens'. The extended schedule of the project reflected the changing economic climate of the 1970s in the wake of the oil crisis of 1973. Roger Burr recalls Humphrey Cripps's close involvement: as at St John's the metal components for the buildings were made in his factory – window frames, handrails, door hinges (actually the same type of hinges as those made for pianos). Moya, who loved working on the detailed design of such items, collaborated with Cripps on the specifications. Jacko Moya also designed a new footbridge to supplement the college's famous 'Mathematical Bridge', a structure to be made entirely of stainless steel tubing formed as hoops, criss-crossed to form a lattice. Charles Weiss had doubts about the practicality of the designs, but Moya developed them with members of the Cambridge engineering faculty and proved them workable. Sadly, the bridge was never constructed. Cripps's business was hit hard by the economic downturn and he was forced to scale back his contributions to the project, completing the phase 2 fit-out with labour drafted in from his factory. He returned to Queens' in the mid 1980s, selecting the architects Bland, Brown & Cole for phase 3, a 'pastiche of the earlier phases' in Roger Burr's view although Julian Bland of Bland, Brown & Cole was, in fact, an ex-employee of Powell & Moya, and had worked on the Queens' scheme. The more recent addition (completed in 2007 to designs by Bland, Brown & Cole) of a top floor, clad in grey-coated metal, to the residential buildings around the central court addressed the continuing need for more accommodation but showed little respect for Powell & Moya's architecture.

Beyond Oxford and Cambridge, which had provided Powell & Moya with outstanding commissions, there were other university projects. For the University of Bristol, the practice designed a School for Advanced Urban Studies and some residential buildings. The former, completed in 1980, was an extension to an existing Georgian building in the Clifton area of the city, designed in a quiet and appropriately subdued reinterpretation of the vernacular, with pitched roofs and rendered walls. It was demolished after the University disposed of the site in the late 1990s. (Powell & Moya had, in fact, explored this theme many years before, in the new dining room for the Bath Academy of Art at Corsham. Set in the garden of an old mansion and completed in 1970, this building featured an exposed timber roof internally and the use of local stone as an external facing. The Academy quit Corsham in the 1980s. The mansion is now flats and Powell & Moya's extension has been demolished.)

More significant than the Bristol project was Powell & Moya's work, extending over more than a decade, for Royal Holloway and Bedford New College (RHBNC), a college of London University located outside the capital at Egham, Surrey. Royal Holloway College (which later absorbed Regent's Park-based Bedford College) was founded by patent-medicine magnate Thomas Holloway as a pioneering women's college. Holloway funded its vast and magnificent premises, completed in 1887 to designs by W. H. Crossland in a fantastically ornate French Renaissance manner. The merger with Bedford College, driven by government spending cuts and announced in 1981, meant that the number of students on the site would double to over 3,000 (15 years later, numbers had topped 5,000) and Powell & Moya was commissioned in 1983 to draw up a masterplan for future development. New development, not all of it especially distinguished, had already occurred on the wooded land north of the Grade I listed Founder's Building and consisted of random, unrelated buildings. Powell & Moya's strategy was to knit these buildings together with new development, eight blocks in total, designed to create intimate, courtyard-like spaces between buildings. Parking was pushed to the edge of the site. Given the imminent move of Bedford from Regent's Park, the focus was on rapid construction – some departments had to occupy temporary, prefabricated buildings for a few years – and economy, since the scheme was largely dependent on

The dining hall at the Bath Academy of Art at Corsham Court, now demolished

University Grants Committee funding. Working with Ove Arup & Partners, Powell & Moya developed a system-building strategy based on standardised components: an in-situ concrete frame with columns at the perimeter (clad in brick) and centre, exposed timber mullions to contain the external-wall system of fibre-cement panels and strip windows, and profiled metal sheeting as a covering for the pitched roofs. All the buildings were between 12 metres and 15 metres in depth (40–50 feet), allowing for a variety of internal layouts and providing ample natural ventilation and daylight. The black-and-white grid of the cladding provided the theme linking the new buildings, and furnished the growing campus with a welcome continuity.

Critic Martin Spring found the RHBNC buildings, completed and occupied during 1986, 'cheap and cheerful rather than elegant', though Stephen Gardiner perceptively saw them as a 'village', nestling under the bulk of Mr Holloway's 'castle'.[27] The aesthetic was neo-vernacular in flavour, as at Bristol, reflecting the rise during the 1970s of a new, user-friendly approach to design seen particularly in the work of Peter Aldington, Edward Cullinan and Richard MacCormac. The college library, completed in 1993,

The Library at Royal Holloway College, completed in 1993, reflects a new direction in Powell & Moya's architecture

occupies a central location on the campus and complements the existing library in the Founder's Building. Constructed in 12 months at a cost of just over £1.8 million, it is, like the other Powell & Moya buildings, a three-storey structure (set into a slope, so that the main entrance is at first-floor level) but deeper in plan than the other blocks (35 x 25 metres / 115 x 82 feet) and externally clad entirely in brick. The top-floor reading room, with its exposed timber roof beams and generous natural lighting, is the finest element in a building that John Haworth (Powell & Moya partner from 1984) fairly describes as 'a building of evident quality achieved within a tight budget'.

From Putney in the early fifties to Egham in the 1990s: Powell & Moya's architectural transformation reflected the rise of Modernism and, equally, its catastrophic decline into unpopularity from the late sixties onwards. If any British practice was able to keep the Modernist flame alight, it was surely Powell & Moya – a practice which had steered clear of the high-rise housing and banal city-centre developer schemes that were increasingly singled out for opprobrium, and had pioneered a modern architecture in tune with context and history. But for Powell & Moya, too, the times were changing.

Notes

1   Ian Nairn, *Modern Buildings in London* (London, 1964), p59.
2   *Architectural Design*, April 1956, p108.
3   *Architectural Association Journal*, March 1956, p214.
4   ibid., p215.
5   'Comprehensive School', *Architects' Journal*, 7 April 1960, p544.
6   *Architectural Review*, March 1974, p130.
7   Nikolaus Pevsner and Elizabeth Williamson, *The Buildings of England, Buckinghamshire* (Harmondsworth, 1994), p317.
8   Philip Powell, 'New grafted on the old (Four additions to Oxford colleges)', *Monumentum*, xi–xii, 1975, p56.
9   J. M. Richards, quoted in Geoffrey Tyack, *Oxford: An Architectural Guide* (Oxford, 1998), p304.
10   Philip Powell, 'Architects' approach to architecture', *RIBA Journal*, March 1966, p126.
11   *New Oxford: A Guide to the Modern City* (Oxford, n.d., c.1963), unpag.
12   Philip Powell, 'New grafted on the old', p58.
13   'Blue Boar Quad', Ar*chitectural Review*, November 1986, p365.
14   Philip Powell, 'New grafted on the old', p59.
15   See 'The search for architects for a new college, 1967', *Wolfson College Record*, 1992–3, pp43–62.
16   ibid., p57. See also Frank Jessup, Wolfson College, Oxford, A Short History (new edn., Oxford, 1999), p17.
17   Geoffrey Tyack, op. cit., p316.
18   Howard Colvin, *Unbuilt Oxford* (New Haven and London, 1983), p187.
19   Nikolaus Pevsner, *The Buildings of England, Cambridgeshire* (2nd edn., Harmondsworth, 1970), p42.
20   St John's College, Cambridge, building committee minutes and correspondence re. Cripps Building in college archives, quoted by permission of the Master, Fellows and Scholars of St John's College.
21   ibid. The archives also contain drawings and perspectives for the project.
22   Philip Powell, 'Architects' approach to architecture', *RIBA Journal*, March 1966, p126.
23   Pevsner, *Cambridgeshire,* p156.
24   Philip Booth and Nicholas Taylor, *Cambridge New Architecture* (3rd edn., London, 1970), p46.
25   Pevsner, *Cambridgeshire*, p138.
26   Stephen Gardiner, 'Masterpiece by the Cam', *The Observer*, 11 May 1980.
27   Martin Spring, 'University challenge', *Building*, 19 September 1986, p39; Stephen Gardiner, 'Black and white', *The Observer*, 24 August 1988.

The administration and residential block at Wexham Park Hospital

CHAPTER FOUR:
A Social Architecture

Looking back at the practice's work after his retirement, Philip Powell wondered
whether Powell & Moya had not done too many hospitals. The technical and operational agenda that inevitably dominates hospital design certainly places limits on
architectural inventiveness. Yet, new hospitals were a key part of the social revolution
ushered in with the rise of the Welfare State after the Second World War. For more
than 40 years, hospital commissions were fundamental to the success of Powell &
Moya, and the practice's achievement in redefining the nature of the institution under-
pinned the subsequent development of hospital architecture in Britain. The starting
point for post-war hospital development was the estate that the newly constituted
National Health Service inherited in 1948: 2,688 hospitals, largely of 19th-century
vintage, run either by the voluntary sector or by local authorities – and many of them in
dire need of investment.

   Despite the emphasis on health care for all contained in Labour's post-war reconstruction programme, it ranked below housing and education as a government priority,
and funds for new hospitals were limited: around £7 million a year from 1948 to 1954.

The admissions unit at Fairmile Hospital, Berkshire, completed in 1956, was Powell & Moya's first hospital project

(From 1954 to 1959, the average annual spend was £20 million; however, this was only a fifth of the funding provided for new schools, and the foundations were thus laid for a saga of chronic under-investment.) During the 1950s and early 1960s, with the Conservatives in power in Britain, the NHS became firmly cemented into a consensus about the relationship between public service and private enterprise – a consensus which it took a Thatcher to shatter. In 1962, Health Minister Enoch Powell launched a hospital-building programme that envisaged 99 new and 134 upgraded hospitals within the next decade at a cost of over £500 million. The programme had to be cut back as costs soared, but the sixties nonetheless saw a boom in hospital building. The Ministry of Health formed its own hospital-design unit, headed first by William Tatton-Brown (who had been Deputy Architect at Hertfordshire, noted for its school-building programme) and later by Howard Goodman, who had done his time in the office of Powell & Moya. The unit was a multi-disciplinary outfit, concerned with cost-planning and management issues as well as the design of buildings. The demand for new health buildings was potentially huge, and certainly politically charged, and a succession of governments looked for ways to make the hospital-building programme more affordable.

Swindon Stage 2 ward block

The staff housing at the Swindon hospital reflected a changing approach to design in the Powell & Moya office

The Princess Margaret Hospital at Swindon, Wiltshire, was Britain's first new post-war hospital. Swindon fell within the territory of the Oxford Regional Hospital Board (RHB), which began planning a new hospital in Swindon – then still a town dominated by its railway works, but a growing place with new industries too – in the late 1940s. A site was found on a ridge to the south of the town, sloping but with excellent views over the Downs. Powell & Moya's involvement began as early as 1951, but it was not until 1956 that the go-ahead was given to start construction of the new hospital. The design of the Swindon hospital was influenced by a major report published by the Nuffield Provincial Hospitals Trust in 1955. This report was the result of six years of work by a multi-disciplinary team, and marked a significant break with the tradition of hospital design rooted in the work of Florence Nightingale a century earlier. Key features of its recommendations were the provision of smaller wards and more single rooms, together with giving every encouragement to patients to become active again as soon as possible – and, in particular, more WCs in order to reduce the use of that Victorian abomination, the bedpan.

While the Swindon project was in gestation, Powell & Moya designed and built (in 1954–6, also for the Oxford RHB) its first hospital scheme: a new admission unit at Fairmile Hospital, a 950-bed mental-health care facility near Wallingford, Berkshire. Fairmile was a typical Victorian institution of the sort still known in the 1950s as 'asylums', pleasantly sited amid green fields outside the town. The brief was to provide two wards (one each for men and women), a treatment wing used by in- and out-patients, a common room and a recreation area. This was a relatively modest project, but it was only the second new hospital building to be authorised by the government since the war and was a significant commission for the architects. It also reflected changing attitudes to mental illness – the ambience was to be 'reassuring and optimistic'. All new patients were admitted to the unit for assessment – being treated there and either discharged, with the possibility of their returning as outpatients, or admitted to the main hospital for more protracted treatment.

In many respects, Fairmile was the precursor of later Powell & Moya hospital projects. The admission unit was an L-shaped, single-storey building, flat-roofed and with generous natural light (although for security reasons, windows – though much larger than those previously seen in mental care facilities, and free of bars – did not fully open). The ward blocks, of the usual cross-wall construction with lightweight infill, had their own enclosed gardens for use by patients – a highly innovative move. The common-room block was distinctive in form, with a dynamically curved roof (on a timber frame) and natural lighting through clerestory windows. A small boiler house serving the unit stood apart from the building.

Sherban Cantacuzino (in what was the first substantial overview of the work of Powell & Moya) was far more impressed by Fairmile than by the houses at Oxshott and Toy's Hill. He particularly liked the boiler house at Fairmile: 'their most successful structures have been the Skylon, the Accumulator Tower at Pimlico, and the small boiler house, set amongst trees, for the Fairmile Hospital extension. These seem to me to be true poetic statements.'[1] Derek Stow, who worked on the project with Bob Henley, recalls the opening by a retired general, who ventured some critical remarks about the architecture – generating a vocal response in its favour by some of the hospital staff present.

The Swindon hospital was constructed in phases: the first, low-rise and completed in 1959, housed mainly outpatients and casualty departments; the second (completed in 1964) was the dominant multi-storey ward block. A maternity unit (1968) and new casualty-and-accident facility (1971) formed part of later development phases. Hostel accommodation for hospital staff was completed in 1961 as part of phase 2. 'Despite its size, the hospital has none of the dehumanizing uniformity so often found in such institutions,' said Pevsner, adding: 'The different architectural character of each part makes the total plan immediately comprehensible.'[2] The *AR* reviewed the first phase in February 1960, noting the intelligent use of the sloping site in order to separate public and internal circulation routes – the upper ground floor served outpatients and visitors, providing access to the wards; the lower ground floor accommodated the movement of food and supplies (and bodies to the mortuary). Major operating theatres, laboratories and supplies departments were also located on the latter level. An underground link provided a connection to the kitchens, which were placed – along with laundry, boiler house, workshops and other service buildings constructed during phase 2 – at the north-east corner of the site. The aesthetic of the first phase at Swindon was spare, almost Miesian, in its austerity.

Richard (later Lord) Llewelyn-Davies (1912–81), who had been the initiator of the Swindon project, was appointed as consulting architect for it, with Peter Skinner heading the Powell & Moya team. The second phase, the ward block, was formally opened in 1966. Llewelyn-Davies compared the diagram of the hospital, based on American models, to 'a matchbox on a muffin'. The matchbox, the ward block, was originally planned to be seven storeys high, but at planning stage it was reduced to four storeys – partly because it had been decided to reduce the total number of beds, partly because children's and maternity beds were now to be located elsewhere in the complex and finally because there were already some doubts as to the efficiency of the multi-storey format for wards. The architectural treatment of the ward block was deliberately distinct from that of the 'muffin' – the horizontal phase 1 structure. Containing over 300 beds, it was faced with pre-cast units on a structural concrete frame. The nurses' flats and nursing school were faced in Cotswold (Sherston) stone – a small group of houses for medical staff were also stone faced, with extensive use of natural timber cladding. The job architects for the houses were Richard Burton and Paul Koralek, and – as in the case of Burton's work at Brasenose College, Oxford – there were hints of the future direction to be taken by the practice of Ahrends Burton Koralek. The hospital boiler house, in contrast, was an impressive pavilion of steel and glass. Swindon was to be one of the most admired of the practice's buildings, a fact which makes its demolition (around the year 2000) all the more regrettable – especially since its replacement lacks any architectural distinction. A serious dearth of proper

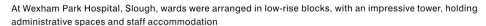

At Wexham Park Hospital, Slough, wards were arranged in low-rise blocks, with an impressive tower, holding administrative spaces and staff accommodation

The reception area in the high-rise block at Wexham Park Hospital was one of Powell & Moya's most impressive features but has now been compromised by alterations

maintenance, combined with a series of insensitive additions and alterations, left the building in poor condition and so mutilated that it could not be considered for listing.

Even as Swindon was under construction, Powell & Moya was commissioned to design another major new hospital, on which Llewelyn-Davies, with his partner John Weeks, was again to act as consultant. (Felix Samuely was commissioned as structural engineer, but died before the project was complete, being succeeded by Frank Newby of the same practice.) The 27-hectare (66-acre) site, flat and rich in mature trees which the architects went to great pains to retain, was at Wexham Park, Slough. Construction began in 1962, and the first phase of the hospital opened in 1966. The generous site made it possible to place all wards in single-storey, pitched-roofed blocks – an earlier plan for a multi-storey ward block was scrapped. Philip Powell's concept was of a hospital laid out around internal 'streets'. Wexham Park, he wrote, was conceived as 'a community, not an imposing institution'; the focus was on the patient.[3] The initial brief was for only 300 beds – less than half the provision at Swindon – with a maximum of 450 beds, so that a single-storey building was more practical. Powell described the building – planned around landscaped, three-sided courtyards, each with L-shaped wards (in form, based on research by the Nuffield Foundation) – as 'a mammoth bungalow'. The aim was to minimise its apparent size and to provide views into enclosed courts, so increasing the sense of intimacy. The diagram, Powell conceded, owed something to Arne Jacobsen's Munkegaard School, completed in 1956, and also to the pre-war school at Richmond, Yorkshire, designed by Denis Clarke Hall, which Powell had much admired. The *AR*, comparing Wexham Park favourably with

At High Wycombe Hospital, wards were accommodated in a multi-storey slab, completed in 1966

High Wycombe Hospital: view of the outpatients department

Llewelyn-Davies and Weeks's Northwick Park Hospital in London, admired 'the sheer humanity of its scale … Slough's humanity is firmly rooted in Philip Powell's personally held conviction that a hospital as a building itself has a duty to provide mental therapy for those who work or stay there.'[4] The 'landmark', provided at Swindon by the ward block, was at Slough an eight-storey tower, containing the hospital's administration and some staff residential accommodation, which formed the hub around which the plan revolved. If the ward blocks typified Powell & Moya's 'humanity', the tower showed their capacity for monumentality, being a forceful design in concrete and glass, topped by a massive water tank. Inside lay one of the practice's most spectacular interiors: a lofty reception area, roofed with a faceted concrete vault supported – as was, indeed, the entire structure of the tower – on four massive pillars, a masterly solution devised by Newby. Alas, the NHS's dismal record at caring for buildings of all periods is all too evident at Wexham Park. The foyer space was ruined in the early 1990s with the crude encasing of the staircase, while elsewhere random additions that involved abandoning the single-storey principle have wrecked the logic of the original plan. When the hospital was considered for listing in 1996 it was rejected by ministers – hospital managers had the temerity to ask Philip Powell to support their objections. The building was designed for possible change and expansion, he said, but had become 'a victim of what I thought was a virtue of the design'.

Derek Stow argues that 'Philip invented the single storey hospital at Slough' (though Powell stressed the importance of Moya's contribution to its design). The 'big idea' behind Wexham Park was clearly Powell's, with Bob Henley heavily involved in the evolution of the designs and Derek Stow as project architect initially (he left Powell & Moya in 1962 to start his own practice). John Cantwell, later a partner in the practice, was also a member of the team.

A far smaller project for Borocourt Hospital in Oxfordshire was very much Jacko's, reflecting his preference for taking on a select number of projects and involving himself heavily in them. The brief called for the addition of a new ward to the hospital, catering for patients with mental-health problems, and occupying Wyfold Court – a flamboyantly Gothic country house of the 1870s, set in extensive grounds. The new building was small, but Moya typically threw his energies into the design, working with Weiss, using long-span concrete beams with the interior lit by clerestory windows. The building was cleverly sunk into the landscape of the park and featured a terrace on which patients could sit out and enjoy the view.

Powell & Moya's two major hospitals of the 1960s, following on from Swindon and Slough, were at High Wycombe and in the suburbs of Manchester at Wythenshawe. The site at High Wycombe (commissioned by the Oxford Regional Health Board) was far from extensive: a long, narrow strip of land on the outskirts of the town. It was occupied by a small Victorian facility, which was to be entirely demolished in phases in order to create a modern general hospital for the town with up to 400 beds. The *AJ* described the site thus: 'a 130yd wide lot on a 1:10 hill bounded on one side by a football stadium and on the other by a major traffic artery; a residential cul-de-sac at the top and a bus garage in one corner at the bottom; not the most appropriate location for a new general hospital – some might say impossible'.[5] Accommodating all that was required on the site was a major challenge.

The confined nature of the site meant that a low-rise development was out of the question. So it was back to the 'matchbox on a muffin' diagram. In the first phase of development, completed in 1966 – maternity and paediatric departments followed in the mid seventies – the wards, with accommodation for 224 patients, were stacked in a six-storey tower, two to each floor, on a triple-height base. High Wycombe was notable for its adoption of the so-called 'racetrack' plan, briefly fashionable in the sixties, in which wards were arranged around the perimeter of a floor with service areas in the centre surrounded by a 'racetrack' access corridor. The 'muffin' contained the operating theatres at upper-ground-floor level, with administration and outpatients at ground level beyond an impressive double-height entrance hall, and all service areas (including kitchens, staff dining room, boiler houses and stores) at lower-ground level. Future phases of development would ascend the slope in the site – a bridge link created in phase 1 to connect to the existing hospital would be extended to serve the maternity and paediatric departments and a second ward block with another 200 beds.

The maternity unit was the first phase of the development of Wythenshawe Hospital in Manchester

Architecturally, the ward tower dominated a highly disciplined composition, recalling the great slab of Swindon. Structurally, this was an innovative building, since beams were omitted and the number of internal columns minimised, with the central core walls used to support the in-situ concrete floors in combination with the pre-cast external columns. The profiled facade was designed to 'combine the attractive characteristics of generous windows with protection from excessive sunlight (and glare)'. A separate development of nurses' flats and hostel in the grounds of the hospital was designed as a tight little village – Philip Powell felt that it should be enjoyable when glimpsed from up the hill, like the rooftops of San Gimignano seen from one of its famous towers. Here again was the aspiration to create an element of delight, so rarely found in most hospital projects but always to the fore in Powell & Moya's work in the field.

The first phase of development at Wythenshawe was a freestanding maternity unit, another disciplined structure in the mould of the ward block at High Wycombe. It was followed by the design for the main hospital, a three-storey structure planned broadly along the lines of Wexham Park but with an internal street that cut across courtyards on the diagonal in order to shorten journeys across the site. Wythenshawe was the first multi-storey hospital to make use of internal 'streets'. This device was also central to the planning of the new military hospital at Woolwich, a project on which Powell & Moya began work in 1971 – the main hospital opened in 1977. This commission also included residential accommodation for officers and ranks of the Royal Army Medical Corps. Using a modular construction system – based on the 'Oxford Method' developed by the Oxford Regional Hospital Board, which reflected an increasing drive to cut the cost of new hospitals – the architects tried to humanise the complex with a series of internal gardens (landscaped by Kenneth Booth), which were large enough to allow extensive views out from the wards. Orange striped awnings shaded windows in summer and provided a strong infusion of colour. The element of delight in the architecture was surprising, perhaps, for a military environment. The entrance hall was accessed over a glazed bridge spanning pools planted with water lilies, and was internally a lofty, daylit space. The residential buildings, too, attempted, perhaps with greater success, to

Ramped 'streets' in the Military Hospital at Woolwich

break away from traditional images of army barracks, with a mix of high- and low-rise housing – the officers in a ten-storey tower, the other ranks in lower blocks around courtyards – not far removed in feel from Powell & Moya's university work. The social club for the other ranks, timber roofed and lit by clerestory windows, resembled more a pleasant village hall than the traditional NAAFI canteen. The hospital is now an NHS institution. Expanded on the basis of a Private Finance Initiative (PFI) scheme, it has replaced the 1960s Greenwich Hospital – like Swindon, a 1960s icon now demolished.

There was more than a hint at Wythenshawe of the increasing pressure from government and the NHS to obtain maximum value for money: thinking about hospital design was equally responding to new ideas about patient care. Should the local general hospital remain the standard model? Could not many outpatient services be farmed out to local health centres, which could also house GP surgeries? The Swindon and Wexham Park projects had seen the architects in pole position, freely exploring the idea of the modern hospital. From the mid seventies on, however, as successive governments strove to come to terms with the economic, social and political traumas triggered by the oil crisis of 1973–4, there was increasing pressure to adopt a standardised approach to the design and construction of hospitals, which would reduce construction and maintenance costs. By 1975, Labour Health Minister David Owen was sounding alarm bells – the hospital building programme was unsustainable, he declared, and major economies were needed. The 'Nucleus' system was the result, created by the

then Department of Health and Social Security (DHSS) and billed as 'the largest and most successful standardized briefing and design system for hospital buildings in the world'.[6] By 1986, over 100 Nucleus schemes, either new hospitals or additions to existing ones, had been completed, were under construction or had reached design stage, representing an investment of over £1.3 billion.

The principle behind Nucleus was the use of a standard cruciform block of around 1,000 square metres (10,760 square feet) as a basic template, to be assembled around internal courtyards. The strategy was one of

Maidstone Hospital was the first of the practice's hospital projects designed on the 'Nucleus' principle phased growth, allowing for a 300-bed hospital in phase 1 to expand to contain up to 900 beds. In general, Nucleus hospitals would be of no more than two storeys, though three storeys were permissible. The advantages of Nucleus for the NHS were obvious – not least, the reduction in the fees paid to architects and other design consultants. For architects, Nucleus appeared to pose a threat on many fronts, primarily that design would no longer be a key consideration other than as a matter of 'dressing up' a standard product. The political imperative behind Nucleus appeared, however, to be unstoppable, and Powell & Moya embraced the programme with apparent enthusiasm.

In 1984, Philip Powell wrote that 'the degree of relief ... which Nucleus offers leaves the architects more time – even within a harsher timetable than is typical for most hospitals – fully to develop the design in its broad aspects – practical, economic and aesthetic – and the details of how to put it together'.[7] The format, of low-rise buildings around enclosed courtyards, was, of course, that which the practice had pioneered at Wexham Park.

The first of Powell & Moya's Nucleus projects was the new £10.8 million general hospital at Maidstone, Kent, commissioned in 1977 and completed (phase 1, with 300 beds) in 1983 with the South East Thames Regional Health Authority and the DHSS as joint client. The project was included in a survey of completed Nucleus schemes published by the DHSS in 1986, in which its quality emerges strongly against a series of other projects of a generally banal architectural standard. On its completion, the Maidstone hospital was reviewed in the *AJ* by Richard Saxon, who declared it 'a recognizably Powell and Moya building, with its horizontal emphasis, slightly Japanese feel, strong monochromatic exterior and nautical touches'.[8] One of the preconditions of any Nucleus scheme was the provision of a flat site, so the first phase of works at Maidstone consisted of levelling the contours on the parcel of land, formerly a farm, adjacent to the existing Oakwood Hospital – excavated soil was used to form mounds in order to screen parking areas.

Saxon felt that Maidstone proved that Nucleus did not lead automatically to architectural sterility: it was 'at least as satisfactory as any new hospital in Britain, and far better than most'.[9] The two-storey buildings were clad in steel panels, like many of the new industrial sheds of the period, mostly in pristine white. Pitched roofs were constructed on wide-span steel trusses, leaving the buildings entirely free of internal columns, and covered with concrete tiles – a central roof valley contained roof lights admitting daylight to the first floor of the ward blocks, while on the operating theatre blocks it housed service ducts. Indeed, the most distinctive feature of the project was its celebration of services, contained in rooftop 'penthouses' and erupting forth in the boiler house, a worthy successor to that at Churchill Gardens, with its four polished flues framed in a red steel gantry emerging from a blue-painted shed. Colour was used throughout the hospital, for example in order to identify wards and reduce the amount of signage. Completed on schedule and at a cost below target, the project demonstrated that financial stringency did not necessarily rule out good architecture.

Powell & Moya was subsequently commissioned to design further wards at

Maidstone and, in 1989, for the Mid-Kent Oncology Centre, a specialist cancer-care facility which opened in 1993. Roger Burr ran the project as partner in charge, with Andrew Mason as project director. The industrial aesthetic of the building was in tune with that of the adjacent hospital – low-rise, with pitched roofs, rendered walls and metal cladding. An element of *joie de vivre* was introduced by the use of a tensioned-fabric canopy over the entrance. Though dealing with serious, sometimes life-threatening, illness, the building, planned around a central garden court, managed to look unthreatening and distinctly non-institutional, pointing the way towards new approaches to the treatment of cancer – reflected not many years later, for example, in the Maggie's Centres designed by Frank Gehry, Zaha Hadid, Richard Rogers and others.

Completed around the same time, and costing about £25 million, Wansbeck Hospital at Ashington, Northumberland, was the other major Nucleus project undertaken by the practice. What was distinctive about Wansbeck was not the architectural form – which simply developed the language of Maidstone – but its emphasis on environmental performance. John Haworth, was a member of a team that had been appointed by the Department of Health the previous year to study the potential for low-energy hospital design. (An earlier research project had generated St Mary's Hospital on the Isle of Wight, designed by Ahrends Burton Koralek as Britain's first low-energy hospital and a brilliant adaptation of the Nucleus model.) The team also included Geoffrey Cundall of Cundall Johnston, subsequently appointed services engineers for Wansbeck. The aspiration at Wansbeck was to reduce energy consumption by 60 per cent in comparison with conventionally designed new hospital buildings. The brief was for a 300-bed facility (much larger than St Mary's).

The plan was straightforward Nucleus. More sombre in appearance than those at Maidstone – appropriately, perhaps, for an exposed site in the North East, just three miles from the North Sea – the buildings were clad in fibre-cement panels on a concrete frame (to create thermal mass), with concrete-tiled roofs. They were heavily insulated, with a continuous airtight plastic membrane built into the walls, and double-glazed, though windows could be opened in summer months – air-conditioning was confined to operating theatres and intensive-care departments. Natural light was provided at the heart of the building, using roof lights. Heat recovery and storage systems, combined-heat-and-power units and the installation of a 100 kW wind turbine – designed to provide 10 per cent of the hospital's annual electricity requirements – completed the low-energy package, its operation overseen by a building energy management system and an energy manager, a post which had not previously existed at any British hospital. Part of the manager's role was to educate the building's users – for example, to accept lights that switched off automatically when a space was unoccupied. Wansbeck won the Green Building of the Year Award in 1994 and confirmed Powell & Moya's reputation as a fertile breeding ground for the development of innovative building technologies.

The Conquest Hospital at Hastings was a commission of 1983. The main phase of the hospital was built between 1986 and 1992, with a team led by Roger Burr and including Andrew Mason and future Powell & Moya partner Paul Newman. For the *AJ*, reviewing the hospital soon after its opening, this was perhaps the last of the general district hospitals, 'the final version of the old style of NHS institution, using design and architecture to reconcile the conflicting expectations now placed on such buildings'. Critic Colin Davies felt that it was an attempt to reconcile two conflicting images of the modern hospital: the high-tech machine for curing people and the cosy, caring 'home from home'.[10]

The first phase contained around half of the 718 beds included in the brief for the completed project. The site was attractive, on a ridge with fine views out to the English

The Mid-Kent Oncology Centre, completed in 1993, was a significant addition to Maidstone Hospital

At Wansbeck Hospital in Northumberland, Powell & Moya pioneered the idea of the low-energy hospital

Channel. Though not strictly a Nucleus hospital, Hastings conformed to the general Nucleus model, with low-rise buildings (a maximum of four storeys, the stepped section reflecting the contours of the site) around landscaped courts and the usual L-shaped wards. The architecture was in the Maidstone mould: pitched roofs covered in concrete tiles, white cladding for the walls, with elements of strong colour – rational but 'humane' (an adjective that was used increasingly in architectural circles from the 1970s on) and slightly Japanese in feel. Energy-saving was very much on the agenda. The form of the building maximised the use of natural light and ventilation, and heat-recovery systems were installed. There was a strategy for commissioning art works for the hospital, developed with the Public Art Development Trust. In short, there was much about the project that was progressive. However, the sheer size of the complex seemed at odds with its worthy attempt at an unintimidating domestic atmosphere, and there were soon complaints that visitors got lost – an upgraded signage system had to be installed. There was a limit, in terms of scale, above which the 'mammoth bungalow' form became impractical.

Nearly all Powell & Moya's hospital projects were for new buildings on cleared or virgin sites, usually on the edge of towns. Great Ormond Street Hospital for Children in London (founded in 1851) was rooted to a site in Bloomsbury which it had occupied since the 19th century – Charles Dickens gave readings to raise funds for the hospital and J. M. Barrie gifted it the copyright to *Peter Pan*. A specialist institution with a global reputation, it had inherited a very mixed bag of buildings. A major rebuilding campaign of the 1930s had been cut short by the outbreak of the Second World War. Bernard Throp of Powell & Moya described its estate as found in 1983, the year of the practice's commission from the hospital:

> a disparate, deteriorating and uncoordinated collection of generally grim and much-abused buildings which had been erected piecemeal over the last 100 years. The tortuous connections between departments, the general inconvenience and the increasing inflexibility generated serious operational problems, reducing the hospital's effectiveness and opportunity for any rational future growth.[11]

The brief to Powell & Moya was, in effect, to create a new modern hospital at the core of the packed site. Existing buildings there – some dating back to the Victorian period and bearing the evidence of wartime bomb damage, others of the 1950s – were to be cleared away. The new building would contain a new main entrance to the hospital, with reception area, cafeteria, shop and an outpatients department. On the five floors above, six operating theatres and a series of specialist departments – for example, a bone-marrow-transfer unit and a neurosurgery ward – were to be housed, with plant on the top floor. Air-conditioning was required for virtually all the treatment areas. Eighty per cent of wards were to have individual cubicles, with facilities for a parent to stay in each room. The cost of the new building was estimated at £42 million, but the government was not prepared to provide more than half of this – the rest had to be raised by an appeal. With a committee chaired by a former Cabinet minister (Lord Prior) and including leading figures from the world

The Variety Club Building at Great Ormond Street Hospital was cleverly slotted into a very constrained site

of business, the appeal closed a year ahead of schedule, having raised £54 million. Work started on site in March 1990, with the demolition of the existing buildings – a complex operation involving the temporary decanting of departments having been completed – and construction of the new building began the following August. As part of the reconstruction, the chapel, completed in 1876 to designs by Edward Middleton Barry, had to be moved. Originally located on the first floor of a Victorian building, it was not only listed but much loved. Encased in a huge box, supported by a concrete cradle on hydraulic jacks, it was lowered onto its new site, just off the central, ground-floor 'street' of the new building. The chapel was given a new roof and externally rendered, with a new foyer area connecting it to the hospital. Its splendidly polychromatic interior – complete with child-size pews – which had been toned down in the 1960s, was restored to its original condition by specialist conservators led by consultant Peter Larkworthy.

The 18,000-square-metre (194,000-square-foot) Variety Club Building, named in honour of one of the hospital's major funding organisations, opened late in 1993. (The use of a prefabricated steel frame with composite floor structures, a strategy widely used for office buildings, speeded the construction process.) Externally largely clad in buff brick, it inevitably makes only a very limited impact on its surroundings, being almost entirely enclosed by other buildings. To the south, however, the new main entrance is approached via a gap between existing buildings – perhaps the glazed canopy that marks it is an inadequate expression of the identity of the institution. Access for ambulances and service vehicles was located on Powis Place to the west.

A glazed panel vaulted corridor provides a top-floor link in the Variety Club building at Great Ormond Street

A glazed canopy provides a new entrance to Great Ormond Street Hospital

The demands of the brief meant that the building had to fill the site available. Each floor was formed as two wings around a central court (a play area at ground level) that brought natural light and fresh air into the centre of the building. Broad, naturally lit corridors ('streets') located along its northern edge on every level connected the new block to other parts of the hospital complex. On the top floor, the corridor was topped by a glazed barrel vault. Great Ormond Street is hardly a typical hospital and its new building was a bespoke structure, tailored to a very constricted site. In the years since its completion, it has worked well and appears to be well liked by its users. The interior design scheme uses both bold colour and contrasting textures to add warmth and interest to wards and circulation spaces, while artworks also feature strongly.

The refurbishment and extension of the Children's Hospital in Birmingham was the last of Powell & Moya's hospital projects, completed after the demise of the practice

Given Powell & Moya's remarkable record of achievement in the field of health buildings, it was ironic that it was a hospital project that led to the demise of the practice in 1997. The new children's hospital in Birmingham was to be one of Powell & Moya's largest projects. A strategic review of health services in the city carried out by the West Midlands Health Authority in 1992–3 led to the closure of the General Hospital on Steelhouse Lane – an exuberant Victorian complex in rich red brick and terracotta, designed by William Henman and completed in 1897. The decision was taken to refurbish and extend the existing building in order to house a 240-bed children's hospital, an enlightened move at a time when many Victorian hospitals were being demolished or converted to residential use. It was also significant that hospital use was retained on a city-centre site with scope for redevelopment – the NHS can ill afford to surrender such sites. In fact, the existing pavilion wards adapted well to modern needs. However, there was a clear need to create new accommodation for operating theatres and other highly serviced treatment departments, and this was successfully slotted in at the core of the site in new buildings which fit comfortably within the Victorian context without deferring to it. Incongruous later additions were 'shaved' off in the process. A reworking of the main entrance featured an elegant glass-and-steel portico added on to the Victorian fabric – the original entrance facade had been destroyed in the 1960s and replaced by an unsightly administration block – while new landscaping around the buildings was designed by Jeremy Lever. Work started on site in May 1996, and the first patients were admitted exactly two years later.

The commission to Powell & Moya from the local NHS trust was secured on the basis of a highly competitive fee bid – 'it was a time when, unless you bid very aggressively, you simply did not get the jobs', John Haworth recalls. The contract made the architects responsible for employing and paying other consultants and contractors. Unfortunately, the funding required for the project was underestimated and the flow of funds from the client was irregular. It was, moreover, a time of rampant inflation. Bernard Throp comments that 'in hindsight, the nature and form of the commission, caught as it was in the frenzy of the government's fee competition policy, contained all the ingredients of inevitable self destruction'. Eventually Powell & Moya was declared technically insolvent: 'Birmingham sank us within a week' is John Haworth's dramatic conclusion.

The hospital was eventually completed, in difficult circumstances but to the original designs, by a team from Bernard Throp's new practice BJT Consulting, and is recognisably a Powell & Moya project. The Birmingham saga was nonetheless a melancholy end to a great practice, which had been at the heart of the British architectural scene for half a century.

Notes

1   Sherban Cantacuzino, 'Powell & Moya', *Architecture and Building*, July 1956, p255.
2   Nikolaus Pevsner, *The Buildings of England, Wiltshire* (2nd, rev. edn., Harmondsworth, 1975), p517.
3   Philip Powell, 'Architects' approach to architecture', *RIBA Journal*, March 1966, p123.
4   *Architectural Review*, May 1970, p337.
5   *Architects' Journal*, 17 April 1968, p824.
6   See Sunand Prasad (ed.), *Changing Hospital Architecture* (London, 2008), pp29–30.
7   Philip Powell quoted in *Building*, 13 January 1984, p42.
8   Richard Saxon, 'Hospital Pacemaker', *Architects' Journal*, 21 September 1983, p56.
9   ibid.
10 Colin Davies, 'General hospitals' final act?' *Architects' Journal*, 4 November 1992, pp41, 49.
11 Bernard Throp, quoted in *Architects' Journal*, 6 April 1994, p32.

CHAPTER FIVE:
Into a New Age

A quarter of a century on from its foundation, Powell & Moya was firmly established as one of Britain's most respected architectural practices, though it had long moved from the leading edge of Modernism to the mainstream. The leading edge was itself being redefined as the apostles of the New Brutalism, the Smithsons and Stirling, were succeeded by the high-tech school of Foster, Rogers and Grimshaw. High-tech gave Modernism a new vitality, and its leading lights were to dominate the British (and, increasingly, the global) architectural scene into the next century. However, the Modern Movement, which had inspired the young Powell and Moya and others of their generation, and whose revolutionary philosophy had rapidly been absorbed into a new orthodoxy, was increasingly under attack. Much of the high-rise housing built under its influence since the Second World War was pilloried as socially and environmentally disastrous. (Churchill Gardens was one of the few large developments that appeared to have developed as a real community.) Pioneers of 'community architecture' such as Walter Segal and Rod Hackney, the latter subsequently to become President of the Royal Institute of British Architects (RIBA), encouraged people to defy the planners and create their own living environments.

The rise of conservation saw thousands of buildings listed and conservation areas designated in order to protect whole districts from redevelopment – the defeat of the Greater London Council's (GLC's) proposals to tear down much of Covent Garden was a landmark victory, which brought together the forces of community and conservation. For some younger architects, orthodox Modernism was not just socially pernicious: it also produced visual monotony and ugliness. There were, however, alternatives including the neo-vernacular of Edward Cullinan and Richard MacCormac (the latter a former assistant at Powell & Moya); and the Postmodern Classicism taken up by Terry Farrell after his break with Grimshaw, which was also the inspiration behind housing schemes by Jeremy Dixon that ushered in the return of the traditional terraced street. By the 1980s, the passionate traditionalism which had lingered on in the work of architects such as McMorran and Whitby, Francis Johnson and Raymond Erith – the latter a friend of Philip Powell, who admired his work – was breaking out of its provincial ghetto.

Opposite: The headquarters for London & Manchester Assurance at Winslade Park, Devon, one of Powell & Moya's few office projects

The 1970s was a trying decade for architects after the boom years of the sixties, as rocketing oil prices brought an economic slowdown and the commercial development sector went into recession. Powell & Moya, with a portfolio consisting largely of public projects, was to some extent protected from the effects of the recession – but every practice in Britain felt its impact.

The decade began well for Powell & Moya with the UK Pavilion at the Osaka Expo of 1970, a project that was generally well received and which seemed in tune with the growing fashion for high-tech. Just a year later, the global careers of Richard Rogers and Renzo Piano were launched with their sensational success in the Pompidou Centre competition. During the early seventies, a series of big new jobs came into Powell & Moya's office: the military hospital at Woolwich; the new buildings funded by Humphrey Cripps at Queens' College, Cambridge; stage 2 of Wythenshawe Hospital; and work at Oundle School (Moya's alma mater). In 1976, the partnership, with the 1974 Royal Gold Medal under its belt, was expanded, with Bernard Throp and John Cantwell joining Powell, Moya and Skinner as full partners – Bob Henley had died in 1973. Two years later, the practice moved (after 14 years in the West End) to its final base, at 21 Upper Cheyne Row, Chelsea.

Although the ethos of the practice was still imbued with the thinking of its founders – left of centre and at home in the public sector, like so many architects who had come to maturity around the time of the Second World War – Powell & Moya was not averse to commercial work. The commission in 1975 to create a new headquarters, accommodating 600 staff, for the London & Manchester Assurance Company at Winslade Manor, close to Exeter, was a congenial one: a bespoke building with a relatively generous budget, for a known end user – far removed from the world of speculative office building. The company had decided to move from premises in Finsbury Square on the fringe of the City of London. It looked at around 130 possible sites, including one in central Exeter, before settling on Winslade Park, close to the M5 motorway and in easy reach of rail and air connections. The site was extremely attractive, with good parkland and mature trees around the manor house, a late 18th-century structure, with some Victorian additions, which had been badly treated during its years of use as a school. Restoration of the historic mansion was a fundamental element of the project and it was converted to house the boardroom and conference and meeting rooms. The restored central hall is a spectacular feature. New interventions were limited to an additional rear stair and the conversion of former service spaces in the basement in order to house conference facilities. The adjacent stable block was converted to accommodate a swimming pool, squash courts and other staff facilities. Undistinguished post-war buildings erected by the school were cleared.

The new buildings were restricted to a maximum height of four storeys and carefully disposed to frame the listed manor house. *The Buildings of England* (1989) describes them as 'self-effacing, in the manner of Powell & Moya's college buildings at Oxford and Cambridge'.[1] In fact, there is a close family resemblance to Cripps Court at Queens' College, Cambridge, the first phase of which was completed in 1975, with its exposed

Exterior of Winslade Park, Devon

The museum of London was designed around the exhibitions which included shop-fronts and other elements of buildings

bush-hammered concrete columns supporting floor slabs terminating in granite-finished fascias, and its deeply recessed windows. In contrast to Queens', however, Winslade boasts shallow pitched roofs incorporating clerestory lights – the top-floor spaces are column-free. Internally, the most impressive feature was the double-height entrance hall. Office spaces were largely open-plan and naturally ventilated. The project demonstrated the potential for adapting a neglected country house to modern office use. Visually, the scheme is a delight, the new buildings complementing the restored house, which is allowed to preside over the whole ensemble – perhaps the nearest parallel in Britain is Edward Cullinan's RMC headquarters at Egham, Surrey (1986–90). In operational terms, Winslade was highly successful. Within a few years, staff numbers had increased by almost 50 per cent and further accommodation was needed. Unfortunately, the client turned to another architect for its design, and the new block completed in 1983 on a separate site to the east is not of the quality of Powell & Moya's work.

A purely speculative office block formed part of the brief for the Museum of London development, on which Powell & Moya began work as early as 1962 – the museum opened in December 1976. After the first scheme was abandoned, a new concept was developed from 1967 onwards. Initially Philip Powell ran the project, assisted by John Campbell, with Bernard Throp subsequently taking charge of it. The London Museum (founded in 1912) had been housed for many years in Kensington Palace, and before that in Lancaster House, until a site was made available, courtesy of the City Corporation, at the west end of London Wall. The deal provided for the City's own collections, which had been displayed in the Royal Exchange, to be merged with those of the London Museum to form the Museum of London.

The London Wall area had been devastated by wartime bombing, and reconstruction began in the mid 1950s to a plan developed by the LCC. Central to the masterplan was the widening of London Wall to form 'Route XI', virtually an urban motorway, with pedestrians consigned to an upper-level walkway – today slowly being demolished – which would in time connect to the Barbican Estate. The plan provided for six office towers, arranged at an oblique angle to the road. By 2009 only three remained – among them Powell & Moya's 13-storey Bastion House, the best of the bunch, frankly Miesian in manner and an uncharacteristic, if competent, work which Philip Powell candidly disliked. The office tower was, however, a non-negotiable element of the brief for the museum scheme.

One major constraint on the project was the requirement to retain the Ironmongers' Hall, a Neo-Tudor building of the 1920s which had – unfortunately, some felt – survived the Blitz. Powell & Moya's first scheme built over the site of the hall, but this option was subsequently dropped after a compulsory purchase order was refused. As a result, the museum as built is divided into two wings framing the hall, with offices and lecture theatre to the west along Aldersgate Street and the galleries and public spaces in a larger wing to the east. The other – dominant – determining factor on the designs was the requirement that the museum be entered from the high-level walkway, so that in the three decades since it opened it has suffered from what appears an inaccessible, even forbidding, location. The *AR* dubbed it 'the most retiring public building in London'.[2] The museum straddles the roundabout at the western end of London Wall – raised up as a massive, dark, brick-faced bastion to high-level walkway level and containing a sunken, multi-level garden with (originally) a restaurant and café. This rotunda, as it was described, was envisaged as a nodal point for the future development of the high-level walkway system, the abandonment of which leaves it looking somewhat pointless. The museum, externally undemonstrative and clad largely in white tiles, was entered from walkway level via an entrance court with a tall pitched, glazed roof, its form recalling that of Victorian market buildings – this space was largely enclosed in 1992 as part of a scheme to create a new shop and café. More recently, an entirely new entrance area has been created to designs by Wilkinson Eyre, and ongoing developments include the complete reconfiguration of the lower galleries, with 'shop window' openings to London Wall.

The constraints of the site generated a complex plan, with galleries on two levels spiralling around a garden court. The galleries were arranged chronologically (with a striking, if controversial, fit-out by Higgins Ney & Partners, conceived as 'a three-dimensional biography' of London) and contained by a solid enclosing wall with just the occasional window allowing views out – to a surviving fragment of the Roman City Wall, for instance, and to St Giles Cripplegate. The two gallery levels were connected by a barrel-vaulted ramp, the most dramatic feature of the interior, with the magnificent Baroque Lord Mayor's coach as an eye-catcher at the bottom of the descent, its setting, in a reflective pool of water, designed by the architects.

The *AR*, usually favourable to the work of Powell & Moya, was highly critical of the Museum of London – 'the supreme virtue of Powell & Moya's brand of architecture is reticence. Not for them the eye-catching architectural gesture,' it commented, adding: 'But here their virtue has let them down: for reticence practised in a harsh and ugly setting leaves harshness and ugliness in command.' (The magazine also published a cutting criticism of the museum's displays by the

One of the most spectacular exhibits in the Museum of London is the Lord Mayor's State Coach, which was set in a reflecting pool

architectural historian John Harris, who 'pined for Kensington Palace'.[3]) Edward Jones
and Christopher Woodward, authors of a well-regarded guide to London architecture,
condemned the building as 'banal and utilitarian'.[4] Yet it is hard to imagine how any
other architect could have done better on such a difficult site, and ironic now to see the
planning orthodoxies that framed the architects' brief comprehensively discredited.
The virtues of the Museum of London are certainly largely internal, but they provide
a careful yet rich setting for the permanent collection, and it is instructive that later
alterations have shown a proper respect for Powell & Moya's work.

Many visitors to the City remain unaware of the existence of the Museum of London
– and miss seeing a remarkable collection. It would be difficult, however, for the millions
who flock to Westminster Abbey to avoid at least a glimpse of the Queen Elizabeth II
Conference Centre, completed in 1986 but commissioned in 1975. The site was that of
the old Westminster Hospital, demolished in the 1930s. After the war, Thomas Tait was
commissioned to revive an earlier design for a new ministry building on the site but this
was subsequently cancelled after work had begun on its foundations. For the next 30
years, the plot stood empty. Proposals for a new government office block there, combined

with a conference centre, by William Whitfield (1965), came to nothing. The project coincided with the publication of the megalomaniacal masterplan by Leslie Martin for the comprehensive redevelopment of Whitehall, which involved the demolition of the Foreign Office and the other ministry buildings at the southern end of the street. Martin advised against Whitfield's scheme and recommended that the conference centre, large in scale with a big hall seating 2,000, occupy the whole site and be a freestanding structure. The abandonment of Martin's plans for Whitehall reflected the increased influence of conservation groups such as the Victorian Society, but his formula for the conference centre influenced the brief given to Powell & Moya by the Property Services Agency (PSA) in 1975, initially simply for a feasibility study. In June 1978, Environment Secretary Peter Shore announced that the project was to go ahead at a projected cost of £15 million. Construction began in 1982 and the building opened in 1986.

The aim was to provide a high-quality facility for international conferences, including those involving Commonwealth heads of state and leaders of the (then) EEC and NATO – these were generally held at Lancaster House, but this was increasingly seen as a lacklustre venue. By implication, given its role and location, the building should exemplify all that was best in contemporary British architecture. A delay to the project had been caused by the 1979 election, a watershed in British politics with the election of Margaret Thatcher's Conservative government. Thatcher's taste in architecture, so far as it existed, tended to the traditional – she disliked the completed Conference Centre and made her views known in no uncertain terms to Philip Powell when she was seated next to him at a Royal Academy dinner, an incident which strengthened Powell's hearty dislike of the Prime Minister and her policies. Thatcher's charismatic Environment Secretary, Michael Heseltine, was not enthused by Powell & Moya's scheme either, but it was no longer practical to cancel it. One significant change was the decision to procure the building by means of a management contract (with Bovis), though the designs had been developed with a traditional competitive tender in view. Nonetheless, the project seems to have proceeded on the basis of an amicable relationship between Bovis and Powell & Moya, whose team was led by partner Bernard Throp. More contentious was the move by the government to transform the Centre into more of a commercial conference facility than a purely public building – an instance of the Thatcherite commitment to privatisation.

Initial ideas for the building are reflected in drawings by both Philip Powell and Jacko Moya, which informed the development of the designs. In the best tradition of the practice, this was to be a highly legible building, with the third level, the main assembly point for conference delegates, boldly cantilevered out with large areas of glazing to provide fine views of the nearby Abbey. The architecture was generated by the structure of the building, which was in brilliant white, bush-hammered concrete (with an aggregate of Cornish granite). 'The Conference Centre … positively flaunts its concrete structure', wrote John Winter approvingly in the *AR*. For Winter, this was a building with a moral: 'if you keep on building thoughtfully and true, you don't have to concern yourself with all the petty fashions propagated in schools of architecture and in the media'.[5] This was clearly a building in the best Powell & Moya tradition – a lineal successor, albeit on a larger scale, to the Oxbridge projects that had been so significant for the practice. Bernard Throp explained that 'the structure is used to give the building its form, and it is this that is so important in its relationship to its illustrious neighbouring buildings. The frame is a vital element giving form to the major internal spaces as well.' The use of lead cladding on the Centre, part of its response to its context, was nothing new: Powell & Moya had used lead in this way on its 1960s additions to Brasenose College, Oxford, and St John's College, Cambridge. (At Brasenose, there had been problems with the lead 'creeping' – by the 1980s, improved technology allowed the material to be used with impunity.) A new element was introduced, however, by the delicately profiled aluminium louvres and stainless-steel hangers that animate the Centre's facades.

Internally, accommodation was arranged so as to 'sandwich' the central conference level, with the main auditorium and press centre occupying the two lower floors and offices and delegate lounges on the top floors. The main (Churchill) auditorium was much smaller than that originally envisaged, with no more than 880 seats, though on the third floor the Whittle and Fleming Rooms could be run together, with the removal of partitions, in order to seat 1,200 people. The interiors of the Centre were less successful, many judged, than its exterior. Powell & Moya had 'played safe' when specifying furniture and fittings, said the *Designers' Journal*. The interior was an 'anodyne muddle', its monotony relieved only by the well-chosen artworks.[6] It was the straightforwardness of the interior that disappointed critics in search of sensational effects: successfully resisting suspended ceilings and other extraneous fit-out elements, the architects allowed the structure of the building an internal expression.

In 1986, the architectural press was preoccupied with the opening of buildings by two of the new-generation stars: Richard Rogers's Lloyd's and Norman Foster's Hong Kong and Shanghai Bank. The Conference Centre received relatively little publicity – 'it has raised scarcely a whisper of protest from the conservationists, Neo-Georgians and Post-modern fogeys', commented the *AR*.[7] The Prince of Wales, who had begun his career as an architectural campaigner with his notorious Hampton Court speech in 1984, made no comment on the Centre either. The most controversial aspect of the building was its cost, which rose to £55 million. (In fact, around 40 per cent of the total cost was accounted for by complex mechanical and electrical services.) The Labour MP Dale Campbell-Savours described the Centre as 'a horrible eyesore … totally out of tune with architectural thinking in the 1980s'. More than 20 years after its completion, the building has not obviously dated and seems a happy and appropriate addition to its context – a fine example of the skill with which Powell & Moya subtly subverted the rationalist prescriptions of Modernism in order to produce romantic and picturesque effects. Leaving aside the alleged shortcomings of its internal arrangements, the Centre is one of a small number of modern buildings in London – Lasdun's Royal College of Physicians and H. T. Cadbury-Brown's Royal College of Art are other examples – that actually enhance their setting without deferring to it.

Though its exterior was designed with security in mind, the Queen Elizabeth II conference centre is anything but intimidating

'Pragmatic rather than monumental', comments *The Buildings of England* on the Conference Centre.[8] 'Pragmatic modernism' was a description of Powell & Moya's work that Philip Powell was fond of. As the anti-Modernist mood swelled in the 1970s and 1980s, the practice avoided widespread censure – most of its buildings seemed to have worn well. By the eighties, even long-established firms with impeccable Modernist credentials, YRM and GMW for example, were taking up the fashion for Postmodernism – one that Powell & Moya firmly resisted. But the 1980s was the decade of contextualism, and the practice's development (for the NatWest Bank) of bank, shops and offices in London's Shaftesbury Avenue, completed in 1981, reflects the mood of the times. The 3,500-square-metre (37,600-square-foot) building efficiently filled the triangular site at the junction with Denman Street. The ground floor was arcaded in order to provide a covered way in front of the shops. The bank was at first-floor level, accessed by means of escalators. In many respects, the building was a characteristic Powell & Moya product, with its concrete frame clearly exposed. There was, however, a slightly whimsical and self-conscious air to the building that irritates even today. Its use of repeated bay windows seems too obviously historicist. The critic Gavin Stamp, however, loved the building: 'sober, rational and ... in harmony with its neighbours ... one of the best modern buildings in London'.[9] Compositionally, it certainly makes a positive contribution to its context – perhaps it is the element of commercial gloss that jars: Powell & Moya did not do that sort of thing.

One project that was certainly out of the normal run of things was the nuclear power station at Heysham, Lancashire – the second on the coastal site. Construction work on Heysham 2 began in 1980, and the station came into operation in 1987. The

Powell & Moya's contribution to the Heysham 2 power station was to break down its perceived bulk with the use of colour

reactor building was a massive concrete structure, 75 metres (250 feet) tall – impossible to hide, but with some potential for amelioration in terms of its impact on Morecambe Bay. This was Powell & Moya's task, and it was achieved with the use of colour: great slabs of green, white and black – and touches of brilliant yellow, red and blue – making the building something more than just a looming hulk.

The retirement of Jacko Moya (in 1990) and Philip Powell (in 1991), both having committed themselves to retire at the age of 70, was obviously a watershed for the firm. Moya had remarried in 1988 and subsequently moved, with his wife Jeannie, to a house in Rye, Sussex, where his great love of gardening emerged to fine effect. He also concentrated increasingly on painting. Holidays were often spent in a remote house on the borders of Tuscany and Liguria. Moya died in 1994 in Powell & Moya's own hospital at Hastings. Powell's obituary for his longstanding partner, 'a great architect and a great friend', was heartfelt:

> from the mid-1940s on I worked closely with him as a partner, designer
> and friend. The two of us were often asked who did what on which jobs;
> who specialized in what; whose idea was such and such a building.
> Agreeably, neither of us – nor others working with us – could give an
> answer, there being no clear answer to give. This, however, was clear: Moya
> was marvellous to work with – not solemn, nor dramatic, nor agonizing,
> but un-pompous, friendly, tolerant, inspiring, inventive and hilarious – a
> catalogue of amiable adjectives.

Powell recalled Moya's extraordinary drawing skills – 'his sketches were not only beautiful … but also honest, understandable and painstaking' – and his passionate concern for detail. He picked out just one project that was entirely Moya's: the Skylon.[10] Roger Burr, who gave a eulogy to a gathering of staff and friends at Powell and Moya's office, recalled that Moya had become for a time in the late sixties 'a mysterious figure occasionally seen, intensely shy, slipping quietly down the back stairs or disappearing in the goods lift'. By the time of the Queens' College, Cambridge, project, however, Moya had re-engaged with the practice and was closely involved at Queens' and with other schemes, remaining to the time of his retirement 'an active member of the practice, contributing whenever an original thought or special detail were sought, and always ready with wise counsel and supportive action'.

Retirement from practice gave Philip Powell scope to pursue his wider interests. He was an active member of the Royal Academy, serving as Treasurer from 1985 to

Drawing by Moya of his garden in Sussex

Moya at work in the office   Hidalgo Moya in later life

1995. His service on the Royal Fine Art Commission – as one of its most respected members – extended over 25 years (1969–94). He also worked assiduously as a trustee of Sir John Soane's Museum, and was active in the campaign to fund a major restoration programme for Soane's masterpiece. Powell was a sought-after member of many competition juries, not least those for the Inland Revenue headquarters in Nottingham (won by Michael Hopkins after the RFAC had rejected an inferior design-and-build scheme) and Tate Modern. He was one of the jury that awarded the proposed Cardiff Bay Opera House to Zaha Hadid (whose work he much admired), only to see her scheme disgracefully abandoned as the result of the lobbying of local politicians and media. After serving briefly as a consultant to Powell & Moya after his retirement, Powell maintained a more distant connection with the firm – 'amicable but ill-defined'. Philip Powell died on 5 May 2003, at the age of 82. At his request, his ashes were scattered in the grounds of the opera house at Glyndebourne, where he had spent many enjoyable evenings.

Powell & Moya's one completed project outside Britain, the Osaka Expo pavilion, was a temporary structure. A distinguished project (1974) for a new British embassy in Tokyo remained unbuilt, despite being redesigned and scaled down in 1980. Not that the practice ignored the possibilities for securing large foreign projects. There were a number of major competition schemes for projects in Britain and abroad, all unsuccessful, including submissions for the Stuttgart Staatsgalerie (1977, won by James Stirling), the BBC Radio Centre (1982, won by Norman Foster), and the European Parliament in Strasbourg (1991, won by Architecture Studio Paris). Describing the winning scheme as 'a stand-alone blob', John Welsh of *Building Design* praised Powell & Moya's proposal for the latter, designed by a team led by partner Paul Newman, for the way that it 'fulfils and expands the brief in an Anglo-Saxon efficiency drive'.[11] (Newman, who became a shareholding director of the Powell Moya Partnership Ltd – as the practice was now known – in 1991, died tragically in an accident in 1997.)

During its last decade or so of existence, the practice remained heavily involved with hospital projects (Great Ormond Street, Hastings, Wansbeck and Maidstone). Work on additions to the expanded campus of Royal Holloway College at Egham continued into the mid 1990s. A new educational project of significance was the Cambridge Regional College, on which the practice began work in 1989. The college was operating, as one of 453 further education colleges in Britain, on 11 sites around Cambridge before it secured

Philip Powell

a large plot at Kings Hedges on the northern edge of the city for a major new development. The site was far removed from the historic confines of St John's and Queens' colleges, where Powell & Moya had worked in the 1960s and 1970s. It was located between the busy dual carriageway of the A14 and a railway line, with housing estates and industrial units as near neighbours, and had been used as a tank depot during the Second World War. The contrast reflected the divisions in British education – cloistered quadrangles for the academic elite, brownfield sites for the masses. In fact, Cambridge in the late eighties was no longer an obscure market town, an adjunct to the University, but a rapidly growing city with new industries, largely technology-based, requiring an increasingly skilled workforce. The Regional College was growing fast and already had over 12,000 full- and part-time students following courses in computer technology, business studies, fashion design and other highly practical subjects. (It was increasingly recognised that the prejudice against 'vocational' training was hampering the growth of the British economy.)

The Cambridge Regional College project was to be constructed in four phases, eventually creating a 9.5-hectare (23-acre) campus with buildings, generally of three storeys, arranged as pavilions along a central mall running east–west across the site. Phase 1 included accommodation for the faculty of business studies, the library, refectory/gym and administrative offices, and was completed at a cost of around £8 million in 1993. The relatively modest budget was reflected in the completed buildings, practical and designed for hard wear, with details kept satisfyingly simple. The client (Cambridgeshire County Council) insisted on the use of brick as an external facing, with pitched roofs – though the latter were hardly a novel feature in Powell & Moya's architecture. As always, the buildings were conceived in tandem with the surrounding

Cambridge Regional College

landscape, which in this instance had to be created (to designs by Jeremy Lever) from virtually nothing – some 30,000 trees were planted. The second phase of the project, completed in 1995, included an administration block, catering and common-room spaces, and a large workshop building with teaching spaces on two levels. The latter was something of a tour de force, featuring a spreading, stainless-steel-clad roof, partly supported on 15-metre (50-foot) high masts, providing a clear 21-metre (70-foot) span internally and allowing for all spaces to benefit from natural light. Powell Moya Partnership director Bernard Stilwell ran the two initial phases of the project and assembled a team that was to form the basis of the new practice he launched after the partnership was wound up in 1997. Bernard Stilwell Architects subsequently completed phase 3 of the project. The emphasis now was ever more on economy, since no funding was available from central government for this phase of development (a linear three-storey block at the western end of the central spine mall, consisting largely of classrooms and studios, plus photographic darkrooms and a drama room). The block took up the vocabulary and structural strategy of the earlier phases of development – a concrete base supporting a superstructure of steel and timber, with bands of brickwork externally and pitched roofs. Internally, the central mall was relocated to the southern edge of the building, where it enjoys views out and serves as an informal gallery for the display of student work. At £3.8 million, including landscaping and car-parking, the building was extremely good value for money.

The Regional College project received a good press. Naomi Stungo of *RIBA Journal*, reviewing phase 2, felt that its 'sensitivity to scale aligns it with the best PMP buildings' and compared it with Churchill Gardens and Mayfield School.[12] Of phase 3, Colin Davies of the *AJ* wrote that it was 'recognizably the inheritor of a long and venerable tradition'. It shared the virtues – 'humane but never cosy, popular but not populist, solid yet elegant, responsive but always in control' – of Powell & Moya's hospital and university projects of the 1950s and 1960s.[13] Others, including some veterans of Powell & Moya's great days, felt that the project's wholehearted adoption of the language of neo-vernacular and critical regionalism marked a break with the traditions of the practice, and that something distinctive had been lost. An alternative view was that the project contained the seeds of a new era in the life of the practice – though, sadly, one that was to be curtailed even before the college was completed.

Reyner Banham's description of Powell & Moya – 'nice, modern and British!' – could be seen as two-edged: was 'niceness' ever an ingredient of great architecture? The practice's reputation and influence – unlike that of Stirling, the Smithsons, Foster or Rogers – never extended beyond Britain. Dramatic gestures were not its forte. Philip Powell confessed that he had a mistrust of 'conscious struggling after originality ... of making things big when they need not be; a mistrust of the attitude which treats any job as a "prestige job"'. Each project, he insisted (in a lecture to the RIBA, given in 1966), 'has an identity of its own and should not, in order to save its designer time and trouble, be allowed to become an arbitrary rehash of one of its predecessors'.[14] Sensitivity to place and a calculated response to the needs of users were fundamental to the work of the practice. Though by no means an uncritical admirer of its work, Ian Nairn, condemning the destruction of Cambridge's King Street by new college developments, including Denys Lasdun's work for Christ's, wrote: 'I have never seen a building of Powell & Moya's that damaged the environment.'[15]

Cambridge Regional College

In common with other Modernist buildings of the post-war decades, those designed by Powell & Moya have not always proved as durable as their architects envisaged. Blue Boar Quad at Christ Church, Oxford, was a potential candidate for demolition following the failure of mechanical services, notably the underfloor heating system, and persistent problems with leaking roofs. Listing at Grade II* ruled out that option and led to the major repair and refurbishment scheme by Purcell Miller Tritton, completed in 2008. Some difficult decisions had to be taken: the replacement of all the original window units, for instance. Yet the refurbishment project has given the buildings a new life, with a state-of-the-art lecture theatre, a facility the college lacked, at basement level. It is hard to imagine the original architects having any qualms about what has been achieved, or questioning the need for any of their buildings to adapt to the requirements of a new age and to address issues that were not to the fore 40 or 50 years ago – disabled access, for example, and environmental sustainability. It is ironic that the sustainable agenda of the early 21st century does not appear to preclude the wasteful demolition of relatively recent buildings with potential for continued use, and salutary to note that no Powell & Moya building – with the exception of the Skylon, the Osaka Pavilion both designed to be temporary structures and a couple of small houses – has suffered this fate. More than 60 years after the practice was founded by two very young and quite inexperienced AA graduates, the buildings of Powell & Moya are being studied and appreciated by a new generation of young architects and enjoyed by those who live, work, play or study in them. 'Humane' is an adjective too freely applied to architecture, but here is one body of work to which it could be attributed with sure conviction.

Notes

1   Nikolaus Pevsner and Bridget Cherry, *The Buildings of England, Devon* (London, 1989), p914.
2   'All glorious within', *Architectural Review*, July 1977, p17.
3   John Harris, 'A curator's view', *Architectural Review*, July 1977, pp21–3.
4   Edward Jones and Christopher Woodward, *A Guide to the Architecture of London* (3rd edn., London, 1992), p149.
5   John Winter, 'Fitting in Westminster', *Architectural Review*, June 1986, p42.
6   Lance Knobel, 'All work and no play', *Designers' Journal*, October 1986, p60.
7   *Architectural Review*, June 1986, p39.
8   Simon Bradley and Nikolaus Pevsner, *The Buildings of England, London 6: Westminster* (New Haven and London, 2003), p272.
9   Gavin Stamp, 'A new avenue for the architects', *The Times*, 31 December 1983.
10 Philip Powell, obituary for Moya in *Architects' Journal*, 11 August 1994, p8.
11 John Welsh, 'Four part harmony', *Building Design,* 6 September 1991, p16.
12 Naomi Stungo, 'Object lesson', *RIBA Journal*, December 1995, p48.
13 Colin Davies, 'Building on precedent', *Architects' Journal*, 23 April 1998, p36.
14 Philip Powell, 'Architects' approach to architecture', *RIBA Journal*, March 1966, p116.
15 Ian Nairn, 'Emperor's new clothes?', *Sunday Times*, 17 October 1971.

List of Works

Introduction

The following list provides a guide to all the buildings and projects undertaken by Powell & Moya. The list of works has been arranged chronologically and includes selected published references, awards, journals, competitions and unexecuted projects.

Key

✳ Award
📖 Journal reference
🏆 Competition
🗷 Unexecuted project

A double asterisk (**) indicates that the building has been demolished.
A single asterisk (*) indicates that it has been drastically altered, sometimes beyond recognition.

Chronological list of selected projects

1946–62

Churchill Gardens housing
Pimlico, London
Client: Westminster City Council

📖 *Architects' Journal*, 7 December 1950, pp481–92

📖 *Architects' Journal*, 2 October 1952, pp406–14

📖 *Architects' Journal*, 24 October 1962, pp967–82

✳ Festival of Britain Award 1951; Civic Trust Awards 1962, 2000
Part-listed Grade II

1947

Masters' houses
Epsom College, Surrey
(Unbuilt project)
Client: Epsom College

One of the nine-storey blocks seen from Churchill Square, with maisonette blocks completed in 1952

1947–9

Houses at Mount Lane**
Chichester, West Sussex
(Collaboration with Michael Powell)
Client: Canon and Mrs Powell &
Commander and Mrs Hogg

📖 *Architects' Journal*, 8 June 1950,
pp716–21

📖 *Architectural Review*, June 1950,
pp397–403
One house extended, 1960; one
demolished

1947–9

Conversion and extension to house at Westgate
Chichester, West Sussex

📖 *Architect and Building News*, 7 April
1950, vol. 197, pp365–6

The Skylon in course of erection in early 1951

1948

Newton-Einstein House
South Kensington, London
(Unbuilt project)

1950–51

Skylon**
South Bank, London
(Project by Hidalgo Moya)
Client: Office of the Lord President
of the Council, Festival of Britain
Committee

1951

Prototype Highworth Houses
Highworth, Hampshire
(Collaboration with Eric Chick)
Client: Highworth Rural District
Council

📖 *Architects' Journal*, 22 November
1951, pp614–18

1951–4

Housing at Lamble Street
Gospel Oak, Camden, London
Client: St Pancras Borough Council

📖 *Architects' Journal*, 21 October 1954,
pp358–62

1951–60

Princess Margaret Hospital**
Swindon, Wiltshire
(Phase 1: Outpatients and Casualty
Departments)
Client: Oxford Regional Hospital
Board

📖 *Architects' Journal*, 11 February 1960,
pp261–72

1952–5

Two houses*
Oxshott, Surrey
Clients: Howell Leadbeater and
Desmond Keeling

📖 *Architects' Journal*, 15 December
1955, pp769–76

1952–6

Mayfield School*
Putney, London
Client: London County Council

📖 *Architects' Journal*, 2 August 1954,
pp163–78

1953

Highworth Houses
Baughurst, Hampshire
(Collaboration with Eric Chick)
Client: Kingsclere Rural District
Council

📖 *Architect and Building News*, 19
November 1955, pp596–8

1953–4

House
Toy's Hill, Westerham, Kent
Clients: Monica and Muriel Anthony

📖 *Architectural Review*, December 1954,
pp358–62
Listed Grade II

1953–6

House**
Leamington Spa, Warwickshire
Client: Mrs Moya

1953–7

Housing at Stokesheath Road
Harlow New Town, Essex
Client: Harlow Development
Corporation

📖 *Architecture and Building*, July 1956,
pp247, 250

1954

Housing at Bishop's Green
near Newbury, Berkshire
Client: Kingsclere and Whitchurch
RDC

📖 *Architecture and Building*, July 1956,
pp250, 255

📖 Paul Mauger, *Buildings in the Country*,
London, Batsford, pp202–7

1954–7

Admissions Unit**
Fairmile Hospital, Wallingford,
Berkshire
Client: Oxford Regional Hospital
Board

📖 *Architects' Journal*, 19 April 1956,
pp385–98

1955–65

Princess Margaret Hospital**
Swindon, Wiltshire
(Phase 2: Ward Block)
Client: Oxford Regional Hospital
Board

📖 *Architects' Journal*, 11 February 1960,
pp261–72

📖 *Architectural Review*, June 1965,
pp426–7

1956–66

Wexham Park Hospital*
Slough, Buckinghamshire
(Collaboration with Llewelyn-Davies,
Weeks and Partners)
Client: Oxford Regional Hospital
Board

📖 *Architects' Journal*, 1 February
1967, pp301–18; 8 February 1967,
pp373–92

✳ RIBA Award 1967

1957–61

New residential buildings at Brasenose College
Oxford (Courts L, M and N)
Client: Brasenose College

📖 *Architect and Building News*, 17
January 1962, pp87–92
Listed Grade II*

1957–78

Alterations to 16 The Little Boltons
Kensington, London
Clients: Philip and Philippa Powell

1958

Naxxar Hospital, Malta
(Unbuilt project)

1958–62

Chichester Festival Theatre
Chichester, West Sussex
Client: Chichester Festival Theatre
Trust

📖 *Architects' Journal*, 4 July 1962,
pp25–40

📖 Leslie Evershed-Martin, *The
Impossible Theatre*, Chichester,
Phillimore, 1971
Listed Grade II*

1961

Transmission Mast
Granada TV Headquarters,
Manchester
Client: Granada TV

1961–4

Staff Houses**
Princess Margaret Hospital, Swindon,
Wiltshire
Client: Oxford Regional Hospital
Board

📖 *Architects' Journal*, 6 January 1965,
pp27–42

1961–6

Wycombe General Hospital
High Wycombe, Buckinghamshire
(Phase 1: Main Hospital Building)
Client: Oxford Regional Health Board

📖 *Architect and Building News*, 12 June
1968, pp890–7

1962–5

Wythenshawe Hospital
Manchester
(Phase 1: Maternity Unit)
Client: Manchester Regional Hospital
Board

1962–6

Cripps Building
St John's College, Cambridge
Client: St John's College

📖 *Architect and Building News*, 13 September 1967, pp447–62

✳ RIBA Award 1967
Currently (2009) under consideration for listing

1962–7

Swimming Baths and Assembly Hall
Upper Richmond Road, Putney, London
Client: London Borough of Wandsworth

📖 *Architects' Journal*, 20 March 1968, pp627–9

✳ RIBA Award 1969

The interior of Putney Baths

1962–76

Museum of London
London Wall, City of London
Client: Corporation of the City of London/London Museum

📖 *Royal Society of Arts Journal*, May 1973, pp404–6

📖 *Architectural Review*, July 1977, pp16–28

✳ RIBA commendation 1979

1963

Princess Margaret Hospital**
Swindon, Wiltshire
(Phase 3: Maternity Unit)

📖 *Architects' Journal*, 30 March 1966, pp837–56

1964

Admission Unit, Borocourt Hospital**
Peppard, near Henley, Oxfordshire
Client: Oxford Regional Health Board

📖 *Architectural Design*, April 1965, pp198–201

1964

22 Portman Square
(including Portman Hotel and Portman Towers), Westminster, London
(Powell & Moya acted as consultant architects, with Michael Rosenauer)
Client: Portman Estate. Reference PA390/5(1-31), RIBA Drawings Collection V&A

1964

Remodelling of 90–1 Tottenham Court Road as own offices
London

1964–8

Blue Boar Quad
Christ Church, Oxford
Client: Christ Church, Oxford

📖 *Architectural Review*, November 1968, pp364–8

📖 Sir Philip Powell, 'New Grafted on the Old (Four Additions to Oxford Colleges)', in *Monumentum*, vol. XI–XII, 1975
Listed Grade II*

1964–8

Christ Church Picture Gallery
Oxford
Client: Christ Church, Oxford

📖 *Architectural Review*, April 1969, pp269–72

✳ *Architectural Design* Project Award 1965; RIBA Award 1969
Listed Grade II*

1964–8

Magpie Lane Annexe
Corpus Christi College, Oxford
Client: Corpus Christi College, Oxford

📖 *Building*, 12 September 1969, pp103–7

1965–71

Housing at Crown Works
Vauxhall, London
Client: Greater London Council

1966

New building for Pitt Rivers Museum
Oxford
(Unbuilt project; collaboration with P.L. Nervi)
Client: University of Oxford

📖 *Architects' Journal*, 27 March 1968, pp639–42

1966–87

Alterations to Tygwyn
Walberswick, Suffolk
Clients: Philip and Philippa Powell

1967–71

Wythenshawe Hospital
Manchester
(Phase 2: Main Hospital Building)
Client: Manchester Regional Hospital Board

1967–73

Plumstead Manor School
Plumstead Common, Woolwich, London
Client: Inner London Education Authority

📖 *Architectural Review*, March 1974, pp126–34

1967–74

Wolfson College, Oxford

📖 *Architectural Review*, October 1974, pp206–20

✳ RIBA Award 1975; Concrete Society Award 1975

1968

Additions to Witanhurst House
West Hill, Camden, London
(Unbuilt project)

1968

Dining Rooms at Bath Academy of Art**
Beechfield House, Corsham, Wiltshire
Client: Bath Academy of Art

📖 *Architectural Review*, April 1971, pp246–50

1968

British Pavilion**
Expo 70, Osaka, Japan
(Collaboration with Takaki and Dodd)
Client: Central Office of Information

📖 *Architects' Journal*, 22 April 1970, pp968–82

1968–75

Housing at Meadow Mews
Lambeth, London
Client: Greater London Council

1969

Medical-student accommodation, library, conference hall and exhibition gallery
King Edward's Hospital, Tolmers Square, Camden, London
(Unbuilt project)
Client: King Edward's Hospital Fund

1969

Building for postgraduate medical students for the King Edward's Hospital at Palace Court
Kensington and Chelsea, London
(Unbuilt project)
Client: King Edward's Hospital Fund for London

1969–70

32–4 Essex Street
Middle Temple, City of London
(Unbuilt project)
Client: Middle Temple

1969–76

Wycombe General Hospital
High Wycombe, Buckinghamshire
(Phase 2: Maternity and Paediatric Wards)
Client: Oxford Regional Health Board

1970–4

British Embassy
Tokyo, Japan
(Unbuilt project)
Client: HM Foreign and Commonwealth Office

1971

Salisbury and Stonehenge Museum
Stonehenge, Wiltshire
(Unbuilt project)
Client: New Sarum Society

📖 *Architects' Journal*, 18 November 1970, pp1178–9

1971

Competition entry for Burrell Museum
Glasgow
(Unbuilt project)
Client: Glasgow City Council

1971–3

Dining Rooms (Bekynton) at Eton College
Buckinghamshire
Client: Eton College

📖 RIBA Journal, November 1976, p456

1971–7

Woolwich Military Hospital
London
(Collaboration with the Public Services Agency and the Department of the Environment)
Client: Ministry of Defence

📖 Building Design, 9 November 1979, pp24–7

1971–82

Cripps Court
Queens' College
Cambridge
Client: Queens' College, Cambridge

📖 Architectural Review, July 1978, pp36–49

📖 RIBA Journal, August 1982, pp35–7

✴ RIBA Award 1982

1972–3

Wembley Synagogue and Old Age Pensioners' Home
Forty Lane, Brent, London
(Unbuilt project)

1972–3

British Embassy
Bonn, Federal Republic of Germany
(Unbuilt project)
Client: HM Foreign and Commonwealth Office

1973–9

New buildings for Oundle School
Northamptonshire
Client: Oundle School

1973–83

Dudley Court
Endell Street, Camden, London
Client: London Borough of Camden

📖 Building Design, 15 April 1983, pp30–1

1974

Alterations and additions to The Imperial Hotel
Howell Road, Exeter, Devon
(Unbuilt project)
Client: London and Manchester Assurance Company

1974–9

London and Manchester Assurance Company Headquarters
Winslade Park, Clyst St Mary, near
Exeter, Devon
(Included alterations and additions to
existing Winslade House)
Client: London and Manchester
Assurance Company

📖 *Building*, 16 January 1976, p83

1975–86

Queen Elizabeth II Conference Centre
Westminster, London
Client: Property Services Agency

📖 *Architectural Review*, June 1986,
pp38–46

1976–9

Institute of Advanced Urban Studies**
Bristol University
Client: University of Bristol

📖 *Architects' Journal*, 15 June 1977,
pp1121–4

📖 *RIBA Journal*, August 1983, p69

1977–81

Additions to Burwalls Residences
Burwalls Road, Bristol
Client: University of Bristol

📖 *Concrete Quarterly*, January–March
1981, pp12–14

1977–82

NatWest Bank
Shaftesbury Avenue, Westminster,
London
Client: National Westminster Bank

📖 *Concrete Quarterly*, April–June 1983,
pp22–5

1977–83

Maidstone District Hospital
Kent
Client: South East Thames Regional
Health Authority and the Department
of Health and Social Security

1978–86

Heysham 2 Power Station
Lancashire
(Powell & Moya acted as consultants)

1980

Jorvik Museum
York
(Unbuilt project)
Client: York Archaeological Trust

1980

Remodelling of crypt at All Hallows
Barking, City of London
(Unbuilt project)
Client: Vicar and Parochial Church
Council of All Hallows

1982

Competition design for Royal Botanical Gardens
Kew, London
(Unbuilt project)
Client: Royal Botanical Gardens

1983

Development Plan for Royal Holloway and Bedford New College
Egham, Surrey
Client: London University

1983–4

Commodity Quay
St Katharine's Dock, Tower Hamlets, London
(Unbuilt project)

1983–6

Laboratories, Arts Building and Residences at Royal Holloway and Bedford New College
Egham, Surrey
Client: London University

📖 *Arup Journal*, Winter 1988–9, pp11–14

1983–92

Conquest Hospital
Hastings, East Sussex
Client: Hastings and Rother NHS Trust

1984–94

Additions to Great Ormond Street Hospital for Sick Children
Bloomsbury, London
Client: Great Ormond Street Hospital

A glazed panel vaulted corridor provides a top-floor link in the Variety Club building at Great Ormond Street

1985–7

Garden Court
Middle Temple, City of London
(Unbuilt project)
Client: Middle Temple

1985–93

Wansbeck District Hospital
Ashington, Northumberland
Client: Cheviot and Wansbeck NHS Trust

📖 *Building*, 21 September 1990, pp56–60

✳ Green Building of the Year Award 1994

1987

National Portrait Gallery Extension
Orange Street, Westminster, London
(Unbuilt project)
Client: National Portrait Gallery

1987–90

St Anne's House Unit for the Elderly and Mentally Ill
Hastings, East Sussex
Client: Hastings and Rother NHS Trust

📖 *Building*, 21 February 1992, pp33–40

1988–94

Library at Royal Holloway and Bedford New College
Egham, Surrey
Client: London University

1989–95 and later

Cambridge Regional College, Kings Hedges
Cambridge
(Project completed by Bernard Stilwell Architects)
Client: Cambridgeshire County Council

📖 *Building Design*, 5 April 1991, p10

1991

Competition entry for European Parliament Building
Strasbourg, France
(Unbuilt project; competition entry placed second)

1992

Neath-Port Talbot District General Hospital
Neath-Port Talbot County
Client: West Glamorgan District Health Authority

📖 *Building Design*, 6 November 1992, p8

1993

Mid-Kent Oncology Centre
Maidstone Hospital, Kent
Client: South East Thames Regional Health Authority and the Department of Health and Social Security

📖 *Architects' Journal*, 20 October 1994, p25

1993–6 and later

Birmingham Children's Hospital
Steelhouse Lane, Birmingham
(Project completed by BJT Consulting)
Client: West Midlands Health Authority

1994

Mildmay Family Care Centre
Tower Hamlets, London
Client: Mildmay Mission Hospital

📖 *Building*, 18 February 1994, pp25–32

Obituary: Sir Philip Powell

Half of the humane modernist architects Powell & Moya

'If my brother had become an accountant, I'd have become an accountant,' said Philip Powell at a meeting last month of DoCoMoMo, the society dedicated to the documentation and conservation of the Modern Movement of which he was honorary president. Instead Michael Powell became an architect, and his brother, five years younger, duly followed him to the Architectural Association.

There Philip Powell met the American Hidalgo ('Jacko') Moya, with whom he formed a partnership. 'Two Powells and one Moya equalled "Powell and Moya",' he explained, although his brother Michael soon left for the more secure world of the London County Council's Schools Division. Michael's early death in 1970 still upset Philip 30 years later.

The Powells' father, Canon A. C. Powell, had been Headmaster of Bedford Modern School and then of Epsom College. Philip Powell was born in Bedford, in 1921, and went to school at Epsom. Despite the shortage of work, the Second World War years were exciting times in which to become an architect. The Architectural Association was evacuated to Hadley Wood, where Powell, Moya and their contemporaries shared a house, and they repeated the experience back in London, where they, their friends, wives and girlfriends moved into the Little Boltons. Powell finally bought the house in 1957.

The regular articulation of the pairs of villas informed the regular rhythms and comfortable proportions of his own work, very different though it was in style. It was there that Powell and Moya drew out their entry to Westminster City council's competition in 1945 for housing in Pimlico, Churchill Gardens. It was the first competition held after the war and, against a strong field and aged only 23 and 24 respectively, Powell and Moya won.

Theirs was a humane modernism, despite the necessarily high densities. The lines of flats, angled to the river, were tempered by a sinuous road curving between them, by jaunty rooftop lift towers, children's playgrounds and brilliant colours. The round glass accumulator tower, which stored waste heat from Battersea Power Station across the river, acted as a further foil, as did the Georgian terrace and Victorian pub the architects insisted on retaining as part of the scheme. Powell and Moya won a Civic Trust Award for the buildings, and also one for the landscaping.

Yet, whereas other architects can be precious about their buildings, Powell was cheerfully content to see changes made, and freely advised Westminster on alterations to the blocks in the 1990s. He combined a genuine modesty with a dry wit and steely intelligence. While Moya immersed himself in design work, Powell could combine design with administration and committee meetings, necessary for a small practice often engrossed for years in the design of large hospitals or university complexes.

Powell & Moya's work personifies the best of post-war architecture. At a time when jobs were scarce, they won another competition, in 1950, for a vertical feature at the Festival of Britain. Each prepared a design, but 'Jacko's felt so right that there was no point going further and we collaborated after that'. The result was 'Skylon', still an abiding image of the festival.

They went on to design more housing, in north London and in Harlow, and a school in Putney. But meanwhile another contemporary from the Architectural Association, John Weeks, was working on hospital planning for the Nuffield Foundation. Asked to recommend an architect for a new hospital at Swindon, he unhesitatingly recommended Powell & Moya as 'the most brilliant firm in the country'.

There began an association with hospital design that was to last into the 1990s, the firm always seeking to make their buildings less intimidating, and scoring a singular success with a hospital at Wexham Park, outside Slough, that was largely a series of single-storey courtyards. 'Hospitals swamped us, rather,' Powell later confessed. For, in a bid to keep the practice small, Powell and Moya routinely turned down many offers of work, or declined to enter prestigious competitions they might easily have won.

Powell and Moya came to maturity with buildings at Oxford and Cambridge universities. This connection began at Brasenose, where they were commissioned 'to fit in, squeeze in, as many rooms as you can without being antisocial about it' into a backyard full of bicycles.

They showed that a British firm could build an accomplished modern design that also harmonised with its historic surroundings at a time when St Catherine's College was courting controversy by employing the Danish master Arne Jacobsen. Like Jacobsen, Powell and Moya also designed all the interior fittings and the landscaping for their scheme.

Powell's 'unique capacity for dealing with difficult people' and for 'adapting modern architecture to an Oxford setting' led to commissions at Christ Church and Wolfson colleges, and at Cambridge. Powell considered the picture gallery at Christ Church his favourite building, 'because I like buildings that you can't see'. This modesty belied the brilliance of Powell & Moya's solution to the difficulty of building on a constricted site hemmed in by some of the finest architecture from the 16th and 18th centuries, of concealing the building behind the Dean's garden and creating a new internal courtyard.

Powell created a similar courtyard at the Museum of London (1971–6), squeezing two levels of exhibition spaces into a tight site constrained by the high walkway of London Wall on one side and Ironmongers' Hall on the other. And at St John's College, Cambridge, Powell and Moya devised an uncompromisingly modern block that sinuously and unashamedly wriggled between its ancient neighbours, somehow enhancing their venerability with its own clean lines and good looks. In 1974 Powell &

Moya became the first practice, rather than individuals, to win the RIBA Gold Medal for architecture.

For many years Powell served as a dedicated member of the Royal Fine Arts Commission, and was deservedly awarded a knighthood in 1975. He was made a Companion of Honour in 1984. He remained a twinkling presence, always willing to answer queries when 'at his best, in the mornings' and to attend events despite his increasing frailty.

Elain Harwood
Independent, 9 May 2003

Obituary: Hidalgo Moya

The architectural practice of Powell & Moya was one of the brightest lights in the years following the Second World War, and for nearly 50 years they continued to product buildings of warmth and humanity, usually with an underlying social purpose.

Other architects were more charismatic and more intellectually rigorous, but few could match the felicity of Powell & Moya's designs. It may be that success at a very young age saved them from the necessity of having to shock which dogged so many of their contemporaries, and the fact that they had found their direction during the 1940s, before the influence of English Brutalism or of American receptiveness, enabled them to avoid some of the least popular facets of modern architecture.

During the Second World War the Architectural Association School of Architecture moved to Barnet. At a time when great buildings were being destroyed rather than created, Moya and other students of an idealistic generation planned their Utopian visions of a post-war world. But the buildings actually constructed in the post-war years were not very exciting; the need was great and quantity was an overriding concern.

In 1946 Jacko Moya, in partnership with his fellow students Michael and Philip Powell, won the competition for Churchill Gardens, Pimlico, comprising 1,800 dwellings, 30 shops, pubs, a nursery school and a library. It was an entire city quarter and the architects were in their mid-twenties. Into a grim world of shortages it brought real architectural quality. What local authority would give such an opportunity today?

Churchill Gardens, built in phases between 1946 and 1962, stretches for 500 metres along the north bank of the Thames. Anyone who wants to catch something of the optimism of Britain after the war should go there. Many of the old buildings on the site had been bombed; the rest were seen as obsolete and were demolished.

The new buildings were mostly nine-storey blocks, set at right angles to the Thames to give views for those set back from the river. These blocks were constructed of concrete and faced in yellow sand-lime bricks, a nod in the direction of the traditional London yellow bricks. The use of brick was something of a surprise, for architects within the modern movement at the time were expected to use materials with less of a handicraft imagery; but Powell and Moya had seen the poor weathering of the pre-war modern buildings in London, and chose a material that would weather well. For the low blocks, which were easier to redecorate, they used the white-painted render of the pre-war modern buildings, and the periodic re-painting of these has ensured that the development has been continually freshened up.

It was not just in its architectural excellence that Churchill Gardens was a break-through. It was technically inventive too, with its 'district' heating, utilising waste heat from Battersea Power Station across the river. Hot water came under the Thames and was stored in a 40-metre-high glass-clad tower and distributed from a pump house designed as a delicious *jeu d'esprit*, a glass box modelled on the glass and steel house Philip Johnson had just completed in Connecticut.

Other housing developments followed. At Lamble Street in Gospel Oak, London, in 1953, a lower density permitted rows of two-storey houses. The clients, St Pancras Borough Council, expressed dismay at this, believing that modern Londoners should live in flats. However , the architects prevailed and, 40 years later, fancy front doors indicate the alacrity with which tenants have used right-to-buy legislation to acquire these desirable houses. A more recent development, in Endell Street, Covent Garden, shows the change in architectural mood over 30 years from the slabs-in-a-park imagery at Churchill Gardens to low buildings on the old street frontage in Covent Garden.

Low-cost housing was necessary and in accord with the practice's ideals, but it was the winning of the competition for the Skylon that brought them fame. This vertical feature for the 1951 Festival site on the South Bank, in London, was a bit of fun and nonsense after years of utilitarian building. It may have been nonsense, but it was a very innovative structure and, working with the engineer Felix Samuely, it was all put together in a very short time.

After the completion of the Skylon, Michael Powell left and Philip Powell and Jacko Moya developed the practice on their own. Philip Powell was the front man and received a knighthood, but it was a practice shared and they jointly won architecture's highest award, the RIBA Gold Medal, in 1974.

In 1956 Powell & Moya completed the Mayfield Comprehensive School in Putney, south-west London, now sadly spoilt by recladding. At a time when system building reigned supreme they showed that conventional construction could be cheaper. As the baby-boom generation grew older, building shifted from schools to universities, and such was the quality of Powell & Moya's work that they were employed by colleges at the leading universities.

The 30 bedrooms built in 1961 for Brasenose College, Oxford, used real stone and real lead to give modern architecture that could hold its own in a traditional setting. This was followed by the Cripps Building for St John's College, Cambridge (1967), where a straight modern plan is bent and staggered to form courtyards and to give intricacy and intimacy to the spaces around it.

Blue Boar Quad at Christ Church, Oxford, places rooms underground to retain the flavour of the spaces and includes one of the most beautiful art galleries in the country. The new Wolfson College, Oxford (1974), and new buildings for Queens' College, Cambridge (1976–8), followed. They were on more open sites, and the designs gain in clarity but lack the contrast of old and new that was such a pleasure in the earlier schemes.

Universities were followed by hospitals. Early Powell & Moya hospitals, such as the Princess Margaret at Swindon (started in 1961), are straight, elegant and spare. Later ones, such as Maidstone District General (1983), are 'user-friendly', with pitched roofs, welcoming entrances and garden courts.

In 1961 Powell & Moya designed the Chichester Theatre, the first professional theatre building in England with an open stage. Twenty years later they designed the Queen Elizabeth II Conference Centre opposite Westminster Abbey, an unashamedly modern building that sits in this most historic site with dignity and harmony. In 1992, Jacko Moya left the practice and retired to his house in Rye.

John Winter
Independent, 11 August 1994

Further Reading

Hidalgo Moya, 'The Return of the "Genius Loci"', *The Listener*, 12 July 1951, pp51–2, 68.

Edward D. Mills, *The New Architecture in Great Britain* (London, 1953), pp55–61 (on the Chichester houses).

Sherban Cantacuzino, 'Powell & Moya', *Architecture and Building*, July 1956, pp246–55.

Architectural Review, February 1960, pp101–9, 'Hospital at Swindon'.

Architects' Journal, 7 April 1960, pp535–44, 'Comprehensive School' (on Mayfield).

Philip Powell, 'Architects' approach to architecture', *RIBA Journal*, March 1966, pp. 116–127.

—— 'New grafted on the old (Four additions to Oxford colleges)', *Monumentum*, 1975, pp55–61 (paper delivered to International Council on Monuments and Sites ICOMOS conference, Budapest, June 1972).

Reyner Banham, 'Nice, modern and British!', *New Society*, 18 July 1974, pp160–1.

RIBA Journal, July 1974, 'Powell and Moya take their Gold', pp24–5

Nicholas Ray, 'Delegate Design', *Architects' Journal*, 15 October 1986, pp55–64 (on the Queen Elizabeth II Conference Centre).

John Welsh, 'Modesty rewarded', *Building Design*, 5 July 1991, p18 (interview with Philip Powell on his retirement).

Wolfson College Record, 1992–3, pp43–62, 'The search for architects for a new college, 1967'.

Dan Cruickshank, 'Cripps Building, St John's College, Cambridge, 1964-1995', *RIBA Journal*, April 1995, pp46–55.

Kenneth Powell, 'An architecture of continuity', *Architects' Journal*, 4 July 1996, pp27–58.

Index

Note: italic page numbers refer to illustrations

Picture Credits

The original source of most of the photographs was the Powell & Moya archive. The author and publisher have made every effort to contact copyright holders and will be happy to correct, in subsequent editions, any errors or omissions that are brought to their attention.

© Christine Ottewill Photography – pp20, 96
© Crown copyright – pp44, 46
© Jeremy Cockayne / Arcaid.co.uk – pp120, 121
© Tim Crocker www.timcrocker.co.uk – p7 (bottom)
James O Davies © English Heritage – ppii, 40, 41, 43, 48, 58, 66 (top), 69 (bottom), 72, 74, 78, 127
John Holdern © Powell & Moya Architects – p8
John R. Pantlin © The Architectural Review – p13
Architecture and Building – p3 (top 1955), 3 (bottom 1956)
The Daily Mail 21/05/1946 – pxii
Punch 14 March 1951 – p36

RIBA Library and Photographs Collection

© RIBA Library and Photographs Collection – pp21, 22 (bottom), 27, 66 (bottom), 73, 75, 81
Architectural Press Archive / © RIBA Library and Photographs Collection – back cover
Brecht-Bienzig Limited / © RIBA Library and Photographs Collection - p61 (both)
Colin Westwood Photography / © RIBA Library and Photographs – pp89, 90
de Burgh Galway / © RIBA Library and Photographs Collection – pp51, 86, 87
Henk Snoek / © RIBA Library and Photographs Collection – pp10, 15, 106, 109 (top), 123
John Donat / © RIBA Library and Photographs Collection – pp53, 59, 62, 63, 64, 67, 69 (top), 77, 95, 109 (bottom)
Millar & Harris / © RIBA Library and Photographs Collection – front cover, p37
Wm J Toomey / © RIBA Library and Photographs Collection – pp50, 52, 68, 94

From the Powell & Moya archive

Alan Williams – pp101, 102, 103, 132
Architectural Design – p9
Bernard Throp – p104
Jeremy Cockayne – p82
John Parker – pp99, 100
John Rawson – p14
Martin Charles – p115
Michael K Bass – p19
Museum of London – p111
Owen Lawrence – pp12 (bottom), 18 (both)

Peter Pitt – pp6, 7, 11, 23, 24 (both), 85
Powell & Moya Architects – ppx, 5, 12 (top), 25, 30, 32, 33, 38, 39, 45, 54 (both), 56 (both), 57, 60, 70, 71, 116 (both), 117, 118 (both), 119
Rodney Todd White – pp35, 124
Sam Lambert – pxvi
Photographer unknown – ppxiv, 2, 22 (top), 26 (both), 65, 84, 91, 92, 112